'I often hear clergy remark tha getting paid. Therein lies the ru if the circumstances of ministi book on making the most of ret retired – and those of us who wi̇ɩɩ ɩᴇᴄɩɾᴇ ᴅᴇɩᴏɾᴇ ɩᴏng – navigate our way through these adventurous waters. The scriptures tell us that old men dream dreams. This book will awaken the dreamer in all of us, showing that retirement is as fulfilling a chapter of life as every other – if we approach it faithfully.'

Stephen Cottrell, Bishop of Chelmsford

'Many ministers dread the thought of retirement, their life so deeply woven into their ministry and work that they fear losing themselves without the busy rush of pastoral ministry. Others cannot wait to lay down responsibilities that they have come to bear with little grace, and found almost too burdensome to carry. Paul Beasley-Murray in this rich book on retirement for ministers helps all those approaching the conclusion of stipendiary ministry, or who find themselves already in that happy state as a 'retired' minister, to take courage and see in this stage of life its huge potential for fruitful discipleship, personal growth and, not least, preparation for life's ending. Whether we look forward to retirement or fear its arrival, this book provides wisdom from one who has already discovered something of which he writes.'

Revd Dr Paul Goodliff, General Secretary of Churches Together in England

'Once again, Paul Beasley-Murray has addressed an important aspect of daily, local ministry – how to end well! Whether you plan to carry on beyond the national retirement age, slow down or stop, Paul points the way to ensure that we do not simply rust. This book urges all of us, as we approach the end of our "official" ministry, to make the most of the new opportunities and challenges offered by a change of pace, place and people. I commend this intensely practical book to anyone approaching retirement and to those who are already retired and wondering what to do with themselves.'

Revd Alun Brookfield, retired priest

'Retirement is not always anticipated with pleasure, nor enjoyed when it arrives. Ministers, being as human as anyone else, can be as confused as others on how to handle it. Paul Beasley-Murray writes compassionately and out of personal experience of the opportunities and challenges that this stage of life presents. Here is very practical advice on preparing for retirement and on how to live creatively through it, combined with rich biblical and theological insights – much-needed pastoral theology for pastors themselves.'

Revd Dr Keith Clements, Baptist minister, former general secretary of the Conference of European Churches

'Paul Beasley-Murray has produced an invaluable aid for ministers of religion, and other people, as they prepare for retirement. It will help some to reflect on their own experiences in coping with the challenges that face those who are retiring from ministry within the church. While Paul has drawn on literature from the USA and elsewhere, much of his book shares personal experiences.'

Revd Dr Richard Jackson, Methodist minister and pioneer (in retirement) of the Cliff College International Training Centre

'Strangely, many of us were surprised and often psychologically unprepared when retirement ambushed us. This is a challenging book to read whichever side of retirement you are. With his usual clarity of thought, breadth of research and a lifetime of experience, the author has raised foundational issues about the third age and not simply given a list of things to do. Here is practical wisdom and a re-imagining of our godly calling. Here is a recentring in Christ to sustain us until our final calling, and a good few sermon illustrations to help us in the meantime.'

The Venerable Nick Mercer, retired archdeacon of London and honorary curate of St Paul's Knightsbridge

'I have been retired for 13 years and have gained new ideas from this refreshing book. Like all the writings of Paul Beasley-Murray, it is thoroughly researched, generously illustrated from personal experience and never shrinks from reflecting on the shadow side of this period of life. The author draws ably on the retirement insights of others and makes plain his volume is not a pattern to be strictly followed, but a personal reflection of a significant journey.'

David Coffey OBE, global ambassador for BMS World Mission and former president of the Baptist World Alliance

'Practical, pastoral, spiritual and biblical, this is such a stimulating guide for retiring clergy and pastors of all denominations. Full of practical wisdom, covering everything from prayer and preaching to exercise, new friendships and being prepared to let go as we reach the next stage of our lives. Paul draws on his wide research into retiring ministers, and the quotations indicate his wide reading and experience.'

Canon Julian Reindorp, retired from Anglican and ecumenical team ministries

'Paul Beasley-Murray's personal reflection on retirement is both enriching and challenging, full of good advice and helpful illustrations. He speaks of older people becoming explorers. It is as Richard Rohr believes, the first part of life is writing the text and the second half is writing the commentary on the text. Paul's explorations do just this.'

Revd Dr John Weaver, Baptist minister and chair of the Board of the International Baptist Theological Studies Centre, Amsterdam

The Bible Reading Fellowship
15 The Chambers, Vineyard
Abingdon OX14 3FE
brf.org.uk

The Bible Reading Fellowship (BRF) is a Registered Charity (233280)

ISBN 978 0 85746 864 2
First published 2020
10 9 8 7 6 5 4 3 2 1 0
All rights reserved

Acknowledgements
Unless otherwise acknowledged, scripture quotations are taken from The New
Revised Standard Version of the Bible, Anglicised edition, copyright © 1989, 1995 by
the Division of Christian Education of the National Council of the Churches of Christ
in the United States of America. Used by permission. All rights reserved.

Scripture quotations marked AV are taken from the Authorised Version of the Bible
(The King James Bible), the rights in which are vested in the Crown, are reproduced
by permission of the Crown's Patentee, Cambridge University Press.

Scripture quotations marked GNB are taken from the Good News Bible published
by The Bible Societies/HarperCollins Publishers Ltd, UK © American Bible Society
1966, 1971, 1976, 1992, used with permission.

Scripture quotations marked NIV are taken from The Holy Bible, New International
Version (Anglicised edition) copyright © 1979, 1984, 2011 by Biblica. Used by
permission of Hodder & Stoughton Publishers, a Hachette UK company. All rights
reserved. 'NIV' is a registered trademark of Biblica. UK trademark number 1448790.

Quotes from 'The Terminus' and 'Retirement: A new beginning' by David Adam,
published by Tim Tilney Ltd, Bristol BS6 5RR, used by kind permission of
David Adam.

Quote from Keith Clements, 'Seven virtues for retired ministers', *Ministry Today* 63
(Spring 2015), pp. 40–42, used by kind permission of Keith Clements.

Every effort has been made to trace and contact copyright owners for material used
in this resource. We apologise for any inadvertent omissions or errors, and would
ask those concerned to contact us so that full acknowledgement can be made in
the future.

A catalogue record for this book is available from the British Library

Printed and bound by CPI Group (UK) Ltd, Croydon CR0 4YY

Make the Most of
RETIREMENT

Paul Beasley-Murray

To the small group of retired ministers
with whom I meet every two weeks
in Ramsden Bellhouse –
in gratitude for the fellowship we enjoy

Contents

III Living a full life

IV Preparing for the final journey

A biographical note

Paul Beasley-Murray read modern languages (French and German) and theology at Jesus College, Cambridge. While completing a PhD in New Testament studies at Manchester University, he trained for the ministry at the Northern Baptist College, Manchester, and at the International Baptist Theological Seminary in Rüschlikon-Zurich. Ordained in 1970, he served with the Baptist Missionary Society in Congo/Zaire, where he taught New Testament and Greek in the Protestant Theological Faculty of the National University. Paul has pastored two churches and was also principal of Spurgeon's College, London.

Paul now worships at Chelmsford Cathedral, chairs the College of Baptist Ministers and leads a fellowship for retired ministers in mid- and south Essex, which he helped to found. He is a patron of the Society of Mary and Martha and of the J's Hospice for young adults and a company member of the Havens Hospices. He has been president of the Rotary Club of Chelmsford Rivermead and in 2018 was made a Paul Harris fellow. In 2018 he became a 'patient volunteer' to help in the selection and training of medical students at Anglia Ruskin University, Chelmsford. In 2019 he became chairman of the Cambridge Society of Essex, an alumni association.

In retirement Paul has published a four-volume guide to ministry, *Living Out the Call* (FeedARead, 2015; revised 2016); updated two booklets on pastoral care, *A Loved One Dies: Help in the first few weeks* and *Happy Ever After?*, a workbook for couples preparing for marriage (College of Baptist Ministers, 2017); edited eight volumes of *Ministry Today UK*; and written his autobiography *This Is My Story: A story of life, faith and ministry* (Wipf and Stock, 2018). He has engaged in three research projects: an article on 'The reading habits of ministers' (*Baptist Quarterly* 49, January 2018); *Retirement Matters for Ministers: A report into a research project into how Baptist ministers experience retirement* (College of Baptist Ministers, 2018); and *Entering New Territory: Why are retired Baptist ministers moving to Anglican churches? What are the underlying theological issues?* (College of Baptist Ministers, 2019). Together with Terry Calkin, he has also written for pastors in the developing world four short books on the four foundations of leadership, which await publishing. Every Thursday he also posts a blog called Church Matters.

Married to Caroline, a past president of the Coroners' Society of England and Wales, they have four married children. In addition to their eight grandchildren, his interests include cooking, travel and parties. See further at **paulbeasleymurray.com**.

Preface

A guide for retired ministers – and others too

This is a guide for retired ministers in general and intended to be free of any denominational bias. I am conscious that, for some, presiding at the Eucharist is at the heart of ministry, while for others it is preaching or pastoring. I have therefore deliberately avoided the use of words such as 'priest', 'pastor' or 'leader', and instead I have spoken of the 'minister', a deliberately neutral term which will hopefully prove acceptable to all readers, whatever their churchmanship.

Retired ministers are different from other people. When they retire, they lose not only their job and status, but also their home, for most have lived in tied accommodation belonging to the church for all of their ministry. They may lose many of their possessions, for in downsizing to a much smaller retirement home they have to get rid of so much. They may lose some of their friends (if not many of their friends, if their last pastorate has been lengthy), for on retirement it is expected for them to move away from the 'parish'. To cap it all, although retired, most feel they cannot escape the call that God has on their life; almost all continue going to church for worship, where they experience another minister leading the services in a way which is not always to their taste.

Yet strangely, although there are many helpful Christian books on retirement,[1] books on retirement written about the special challenges which ministers face are rare. What is more, the only books on ministerial retirement I have come across have been written from a North American perspective.[2] True, within a UK context there have been articles published on ministerial retirement;[3] and some years ago James Taylor, a Scottish Baptist minister, devoted one-third of a more general book on ministry to retirement issues.[4] However, no book has been written on ministerial retirement from a distinctively British perspective. So, as far as I am aware, this book is a first!

Hopefully this book will help to address the imbalance which is present on some retirement courses for ministers, where much of the content seems to be devoted to practical issues like pensions and housing, with little reference to all the other issues which are part of the ministerial retirement experience. Perhaps this is why so many ministers appear to be largely unprepared for retirement.[5]

Although the book's focus is on ministers, I would like to think that there is much within it that is relevant to any Christian who is retired or moving towards retirement. For the call to discipleship does not cease the moment we retire – God still has a call on every Christian's life. As Os Guinness wrote:

> As followers of Christ we are called to be before we are called to do and our calling both to be and to do is fulfilled only in being called to him. So calling should not only precede career but outlast it too. Vocations never end, even when occupations do. We may retire from our jobs, but never from our calling. We may at times be unemployed, but no one ever becomes uncalled.[6]

Furthermore, the ageing, process together with its limitations and challenges, is common to us all, whether ordained or not.

A guide with origins in a research project

This book has its origins in a research project to discover how ministers experience retirement. James Taylor in *Pastors under Pressure* had painted a somewhat negative picture of retirement. Reading it four years into retirement, it was a picture I did not recognise.

My experience of retirement had been very positive. But was my experience of retirement less typical than his? This was something I wished to explore. As a result I engaged in some qualitative research conducted within the context of a series of face-to-face interviews, supported by some limited quantitative research based on a lengthy questionnaire. The detailed results of this research are found in my book *Retirement Matters for Ministers*.

In response to the question 'What is the best thing you enjoy about retirement?', freedom, together with variations on the theme, was the only or almost exclusive reply of 87% of respondents: 'freedom to serve God on my own terms'; 'freedom and a more relaxed life'; 'freedom to choose what I do'; 'freedom to say "no"'; 'freedom to go and watch Essex County Cricket'; 'not having responsibility'; 'freedom from pressure'; 'flexibility'; 'freedom from "must do" pressure'; 'free – not having to go out every evening'; 'space to read a novel, to think, to meet regularly with friends and talk'; 'free to have time for family and going away a lot'; 'freedom from time pressure'; 'freedom to do things'; 'freedom to travel'.[7]

There were similar positive responses to the question 'What emotions did you feel in the first months of retirement?' Relief was the overwhelming emotion, mentioned by just over half of the respondents. Thank God, the pressures of ministry had ceased – 'no more meetings', wrote one minister; 'no longer having to bear the responsibility', said another.

Joy was mentioned by two-fifths of the respondents. Although this was for the most part not defined, several mentioned the joy of 'being able to spend more time with my wife'; another 'not having to go out to meetings every night'; yet another the joy of 'mission completed'; and another 'the sense of a new beginning'.

However, there were also less positive responses. Loneliness was mentioned by a good number. Depression or 'deep sadness' was highlighted by others. In part this related to 'disappointment of being disposed of' and was symptomatic of the loss of role.[8] However, it may well be that the sadness related to not being able to complete all that they felt God had called them to do.[9]

When asked to give their 'general reflections' on their experience of retirement, it was clear that although most respondents had a good experience of retirement, not all did:

- Almost three-quarters of those surveyed were 'happy to be retired'; but the inference is that one-quarter of them were apparently not happy.

- Just under two-thirds said that 'retirement has given me new opportunities to serve God'; but the inference is that the other third had not taken these new opportunities. By contrast, one in ten said they were 'still searching for purpose'.

- Just over half were 'glad to pursue new interests outside the church'; but the inference is that the other half were not pursuing any new interests outside the church.

- Under half of the respondents viewed retirement as 'an opportunity to relax and rest'. The inference is that the other 55% did not think of retirement 'as the "Sabbath" of life; the evening's rest awaiting us at the end of a lifetime of work and responsibility'.[10] Indeed, one-fifth said that 'in retirement they were busier than ever'. In the light of past surveys in which the average working week for many ministers can exceed 60 hours a week, such a statement is perhaps questionable.[11] On the other hand, maybe the statement is not to be taken literally, but is simply an indication that for many life in retirement is 'full'.

- Just over a third agreed that 'retirement is a great adventure'. Presumably the other two-thirds did not agree.

- Around one in seven felt that 'retirement has led to a restriction in life'. Although for some respondents the restriction was linked with increasing old age, for others in this group the whole experience of retirement was viewed as restrictive, for they also described retirement as 'boring'.

A guide rooted in my positive experience of ministry and retirement

In the words of the psalmist, 'the boundary lines have fallen for me in pleasant places' (Psalm 16:6): God has been good to me in the way he has 'marked out' the parameters of my life. Or, to use another expression of the psalmist, God has blessed me by setting my feet 'in a broad place' (Psalm 18:19; 31:8). I have known much happiness and fulfilment in ministry; I have also enjoyed the new freedoms and opportunities of 'retirement'. As I said in my autobiography, *This Is My Story*, 'Ministry for me has been an amazing privilege. The good times have far outweighed the difficulties I encountered. I have been surrounded by people who have loved me, encouraged me, supported me, and time and again have been patient with me. I have been undeservedly blessed – and for that I am grateful.'[12]

Yet, as my autobiography makes clear, I have also known tough times, when God seemed to be absent and life seemed to be unfair. I mention this because a friend was concerned about my positive approach: some, he said, might respond, 'It's alright for him to say that, but if he had had my experience or had my current situation, he might think differently.' As with the problem of suffering, there is no place for glib answers. To those who feel depressed or forgotten, I can only say that as in ministry, so now in our retirement, we are called to follow in the steps of Jesus who has promised that the day will come when whoever serves him will be honoured by his Father (John 12:26). Yes, we will be rewarded for our labours, but not necessarily in this life. To judge what is a 'successful' life demands the perspective of eternity.

Introduction:
facing the challenge of retirement

For everything there is a season.
ECCLESIASTES 3:1

I was ordained to Baptist ministry on Saturday 10 October 1970. Forty-three years later, on Sunday 14 March 2014, I retired from stipendiary ministry at the age of 70.

At first I struggled to call myself 'retired'. Indeed, for the first few months I shied away from using the 'R' word and tended to say that I had 'stepped down from leading the church'. The word 'retirement' has such negative connotations.[13] Perhaps not surprisingly, Ernest Hemingway said that 'retirement is the filthiest word in the language'.[14] According to the *Shorter Oxford English Dictionary*, to 'retire' means to 'withdraw', to 'retreat', to 'give ground', to 'cease to compete'. In one sense that is true: retirement does involve a leaving of office or of employment. Yet retirement is also about new beginnings and new opportunities. It is about a new life. Retirement is part of God's rhythm for our lives – 'for everything there is a season' (Ecclesiastes 3:1).

Indeed, on the basis of the imagery of Ecclesiastes 3:1–8, in a sermon preached on the occasion of a friend retiring after 33 years as leader of a large Baptist church in Hamburg, I said:

There is a time to lead, and a time to be led.
There is a time to serve, and a time to be served.
There is a time to be known, and a time to be unknown.
There is a time to do, and a time to be.

I now think that the seasons of ministry are not binary, but threefold in number. Ministry begins with the season of springtime – the years of youthful energy and enthusiasm (25–45); then comes summertime – the years of growing maturity (45–60); and later comes autumn – the years of wisdom and fruitfulness (60-plus), which mark not just the concluding years of stipendiary ministry but also the years of retirement.[15] To describe retirement as 'the winter of ministry' is surely wrong.[16] Drawing upon the opening line of John Keats' poem 'To Autumn', I suggest that it is the season of 'mellow fruitfulness'.[17]

Retirement also marks the beginning of 'Freedom Day', when we are free to be ourselves.[18] Much as I found it hard saying goodbye to Central Baptist Church, Chelmsford, it was great to say goodbye to being out most nights of the week, either attending meetings or visiting people in their homes. Much as I loved to preach, and still do, I am happy to sit in the pew and listen to someone else preach. Much as I loved running a church, it is a relief to be no longer responsible for one – I am delighted the 'struggle' is over. I do not hanker to remain a member of the 'ruling generation'.[19]

Nor do I mind that I am no longer at the centre of a church's life, for I have a strong enough sense of my own identity to be content on the periphery. The one thing I did find difficult was not interacting with people throughout the day. I am a social being, and it felt strange working alone at home, rather than working from a busy church centre. I missed people.

Overall, the losses I have experienced are counterbalanced by the gains. Retirement offers new opportunities and new challenges. Retirement can be an exciting period of life. Apart from childhood, it is the most dynamic stage of life. Change follows change. According to Nathan and Beth Davis, 'It is a never-ending process partnering with God to refocus yourself, constantly discovering avenues in which God can use you, and constantly learning new, deeper ways to facilitate communion with God and others.'[20]

My wife, Caroline, had a grandmother who used to quote regularly some lines of Robert Browning's 'Rabbi Ben Ezra':

Grow old along with me!
The best is yet to be,
The last of life, for which the first was made:
Our times are in His hand
Who saith, 'A whole I planned,
Youth shows but half; trust God: see all, nor be afraid!'[21]

At the time I thought it was somewhat quaint. Now that I have joined the ranks of the retired, I thoroughly agree. Retirement offers an opportunity to be more alive than ever. Or as James Woodward said, 'There is a difference between living and being alive. Growing older is about adding life to years rather than just adding years to our lives.'[22]

As I reflect on retirement, a poem which sums up my experience so far is 'The Terminus', written by David Adam, a former vicar of the Holy Island Lindisfarne:

The Terminus is not where we stay,
It is the beginning of a new journey.
It is where we reach out beyond,
where we experience new adventures.
It is where we get off to enter new territory,
to explore new horizons, to extend our whole being.
It is a place touching the future.
It opens up new vistas.
It is the gateway to eternity.[23]

Retirement is about 'the beginning of a new journey'. There is nothing static about retirement. Retirement is not about sitting in the waiting room of death, but it is an opportunity to discover new ways of living that fullness of life that Jesus promised (John 10:10). True, the opportunity needs to be seized. Sitting around in the 'terminus', watching daytime TV, is a diminishment of life. For me, retirement opens the door to further growth and self-development. The words of Sir Francis Bacon are pertinent to retirement: 'A wise man will make more opportunities than he finds.'[24]

1

Beginning a new journey

1

Enjoy the new adventure

By faith Abraham… set out, not knowing where he was going.
HEBREWS 11:8

Retirement, wrote David Adam, is about experiencing 'new adventures'. I love the term 'adventure'. It reminds me of my childhood, when I devoured Enid Blyton's stories of the Secret Seven and the Famous Five. Indeed, it has been said that growing old successfully requires 'the curiosity of a five-year-old and the confidence of a teenager. There is nothing we can't do if we want to do it.'[25] Growing old can be an exciting business!

Adventures by definition carry an element of risk: 'It's something you've got to go with daring', said John Hinde, who on ending his career at Lloyds of London set up a new farming community. There are times when we shall get things wrong and perhaps have to start again. But even so, let's not be afraid to push the boundaries and see what is possible. As T.S. Eliot suggested, old men ought to be explorers.[26]

In this book I want to encourage my fellow retired ministers to be positive about their new stage of life. The pace may have changed, but as the 85-year-old Caleb discovered, there are still 'mountains' to climb (Joshua 14:12, AV). Or as Richard Morgan put it, Caleb 'asked for a challenge, not a cushion. He wanted more adventures in his "retirement" years.'[27] There is a future to look forward to, and not just a past to look back upon.

True, in some ways the journey into retirement can feel scary. There have been times when I have felt like Abraham, who in his mid-70s 'by faith… set out, not knowing where he was going' (Hebrews 11:8). Just as the years of active ministry held all sorts of surprises, so too do the years of retirement. God alone knows how many years lie ahead of us; God alone knows how long we shall be blessed with health and strength. But one thing we do know: God promises to be with us, so he will continue to be with us in all the twists and turns of the journey. In that regard, we need to claim Psalm 121 for ourselves: 'I lift up my eyes to the hills – from where will my help come? My help comes from the Lord, who made heaven and earth' (Psalm 121:1–2).

Retired ministers need to have the spirit of Helen Keller, the blind-deaf American social activist and author, who in her book *Let Us Have Faith*, in the chapter entitled 'Faith fears not', declared in bold print: 'Life is either a daring adventure or nothing.'[28] Or as we might say in this context, 'Retirement is either a daring adventure or nothing.' So long as God gives us breath we are called to rise to the challenge of living for him and with him. There will be tough times. Life must have been incredibly tough for Helen Keller. But there will be many good times, too. So let's be determined to enjoy the new adventure which is ours.

2

Resolve to grow

The days of our life are seventy years, or perhaps eighty, if we are strong… So teach us to count our days that we may gain a wise heart.
PSALM 90:10, 12

There are various ways of categorising old age. In my 20s I thought that anybody over the age of 40 was old. From the perspective of ancient society, I was right. The Romans called a man under 40 a *iuvenis*, i.e. a young man ('juvenile'), while a man over 40 was called a *senex*, i.e. an old man ('senile'). In the ancient world, there was no such thing as middle age.

Some years ago I was asked to speak at Spring Harvest on 'Faith at Fifty', as if 50 marked the transition into old age. That accords with the thinking of Victor Hugo: 'Forty is the old age of youth; fifty the youth of old age.'[29]

People used to link their definition of old age with the statutory retirement age, but since October 2011 there is no mandatory age for retirement in the UK. The state pension age for both men and women will be 66 in October 2020. At the time of writing, the government is planning further increases, which will raise the state pension age from 66 to 67 between 2026 and 2028. But to define old people as 'pensioners' is not helpful, for that is too broad a term. There are various stages within old age.

Paul Stevens adopted three subcategories for old age: 'young olds' are 60–69; 'old olds' are 70–79; and 'oldest olds' are 80-plus.[30] The World Health Organization, recognising that the term 'old' is insufficient, suggested that 'the elderly' are 60–74, while 'the aged' are 75 and above.

Frankly, I find these categories demeaning. Although my energy levels are not the same as when I was 21, nonetheless at the age of 75 I don't feel an 'old old'; I certainly don't feel 'elderly', nor am I 'aged'. I therefore read with great interest the suggestion of Camilla Cavendish that old age for most people does not begin until they hit 74 – up until 74, people are 'middle-aged'.[31] The fact is that the stages of life are changing – primarily for health reasons. Cavendish notes that in England, the proportion of over-65s with any kind of impairment has been falling for two decades. In America, three-quarters of people under 75 have no problem with hearing or vision, no difficulty walking and no form of cognitive impairment. Step up a generation, to those aged 75 to 85, and half have none of these disabilities. Significantly only one in six people over 80 have dementia.[32]

Not surprisingly, therefore, many older people don't really feel old. Indeed, in a survey of people over 80, conducted over 30 years ago, although 53% admitted they were old, 36% reported that they considered themselves middle-aged and 11% young.[33] According to American research anthropologist Sharon Kaufmann, 'When old people talk about themselves, they express a sense of self that's ageless – an identity that maintains continuity despite the physiological and social changes that come with age.'[34]

One way of looking at the ageing process is to divide life into four stages or 'ages':

1 First age: childhood.
2 Second age: paid work and family raising.
3 Third age (sometimes called the 'golden age'): active independent

life beyond child-rearing and work. This can be a very active period of life. Many are active in pursuing all kinds of further education in a variety of groups and organisations, such as the University of the Third Age. Others are active as volunteers. Many churches are dependent upon 'third-agers' to support many of their activities.

4 Fourth age: the age of eventual dependence, often very short.

An imaginative approach to the life cycle of older people was developed by Tim Stafford, who broke the years beyond 65 into seven 'days of the week of old age':[35]

- The First Day – Freedom Day – begins with retirement, which introduces the life of leisure.
- The Second Day – Day of Reflection – leads an elderly person to begin meditating on their life.
- The Third Day – Widow's Day – comes with the loss of a spouse.
- The Fourth Day – Role-Reversal Day – begins when an older person needs frequent help to manage.
- The Fifth Day – Dependence Day – comes when a person must lean on others for basic needs.
- The Sixth Day – Farewell Day – is the period of preparing for death.
- The Seventh Day – Sabbath Day – is the day of worship, the day of rest.

However, what matters in the end is not the years of age but our attitude. 'You do not grow old', it has been said; rather, 'when you cease to grow, you are old'. Or in the words of Eugene Bianchi, 'The greatest tragedy for a religious person is not being a sinner, but the embracing of stagnation, the refusal to grow.'[36] We are not just human 'beings', we are to be human 'becomings'.[37] It has been said that 'if we can look back on our Christian lives five years ago and see no changes that have now taken place, no experiences from which we have learned, then… we have stagnated'.[38]

We never grow too old to learn. As Gordon Harris argued, 'Jethro, the father-in-law of Moses, Moses himself, Joshua, Caleb, Barzillai, the older counsellors of Rehoboam, Simeon, Anna, and early Jewish rabbis represent the best in lifelong learning. Lessons from these examples, undergirded by a high view of the potential of God's greatest creation, present a demanding challenge for growth to the older generation.'[39] I shall never forget meeting a distinguished American emeritus professor in church history, then in his late 70s, who at one point in our conversation said, 'Yes, in that particular area I've still got a lot of growing to do.' That challenged me to ask myself, 'When I am in my late 70s will I still be in the business of growing?'

Now is not the moment to write our obituary for the newspaper, nor is it the time to create an epitaph for our tombstone. We are not 'have-beens', but are still in the process of becoming the people God wants us to be. So let's resolve to be true to our calling by resolving to grow, rather than just grow old!

3

Dream dreams

Without a vision, the people perish.

PROVERBS 29:18 (AV)

At Pentecost Peter spoke of old men dreaming dreams (Acts 2:17). Growing old is an opportunity not only to dream dreams, but also to realise some of our dreams. So let me encourage you to do precisely that. In this regard, remember Proverbs 29:18: 'Without a vision, the people perish' (AV). I believe these words can be applied to the life of the retired: without a vision, our retirement will not be all that it could be.

At my last appraisal as a working minister I set out a list of aims for the first year of retirement. Overall, I said: 'Enjoy the freedom which this new stage of life brings! Continue to grow and develop as a person. Find new ways of serving God and sharing my faith.' I then listed a number of concrete goals, which included:

- Expand my spiritual life: develop a new daily pattern for reading and praying.
- Make the most of cultural opportunities: attend the lunchtime concerts at the cathedral; diarise monthly visits to London, Cambridge, etc.
- Keep abreast theologically: join the Cathedral Theological Society; develop a discipline of reading and study; continue to review books for *Ministry Today UK*.
- Keep alert mentally: join a book club? University of the Third Age?
- Keep fit: develop a disciplined regime of walking and swimming.

- Enjoy family life: visit our children and work on relationships with grandchildren; keep in touch with family (both the immediate and the wider family) through email and Skype.
- Support Caroline as she develops her new role as H.M. senior coroner for the whole of the county.
- Cultivate relationships: renew old friendships; develop a new social network; learn new culinary skills; host fortnightly supper parties.
- Develop new IT skills: learn how to scan, make PDFs, create hyperlinks, so that I can manage and develop my website.
- Engage with others: maintain my weekly blog; interact with websites, etc.
- Produce a new lecture course on ministry.
- Continue to write: write a 'magnum opus'; write up my ministry; continue to write articles for *Ministry Today UK*.
- Engage in ministry: expand the work of *Ministry Today UK*; develop the work of the College of Baptist Ministers; mentor new ministers?
- Travel.

I ended this list with the caveat '*Deo Volente*, God willing! So much depends on health.'

I strongly believe that it is important to dream and to make plans in the light of those dreams. This conviction was reinforced for me when, within a month or so of having retired, Caroline and I were having supper with two retired friends, both of whom are very involved in the life of the community. Out of the blue, the husband asked, 'Paul, do you have a three- or five-year plan for the next stage of your life?' I had plans, but I confess that I had not developed a three-year plan. On reflection, I think there is much to be said for developing a rolling three-year plan, recognising that it is always 'if the Lord wishes' (James 4:15). So I have begun to set myself goals. I can't pretend that I have so far achieved all my goals. A good number of the goals have changed. However, the principle of dreaming dreams and then seeking to realise them is, I believe, sound.

Even in retirement, there is a place for dreaming. For retirement is not a destination; it is simply a time of redirection. We are only truly old when regrets take the place of our dreams.[40]

4

Find a mentor or soul friend

[Barnabas] was a good man, full of the Holy Spirit and of faith... [He] went to Tarsus to look for Saul.
ACTS 11:24–25

When we first began in ministry, there was so much we did not know. At that stage all of us needed some kind of Barnabas figure who was there to encourage and to help. By contrast, by the time we finished in ministry, we were old hands, who knew how to handle the ropes – and no doubt many of us were Barnabas figures to others.

Entering into retirement is a bit like beginning ministry: there are so many things we do not know. What is more, we are now very much on our own: we have no senior figure (church warden or church secretary) to advise us. All the more reason to look around for a mentor or soul friend: perhaps somebody who has already begun the journey, an older retired minister who can be there for us.[41] There is a lot to be said for finding such a mentor or soul friend a year or so before retirement. Those final twelve months of stipendiary ministry and the first twelve months of retirement can be spiritually challenging – this is just the time when we could benefit from a wise and experienced friend who has already begun to walk the retirement path.[42] To my surprise, however, there seems to be reluctance on the part of retired ministers to see the benefit of having a person to input into their life. In my research on how ministers experience retirement, only a third saw any need for a mentor or somebody to accompany them on their spiritual journey.[43]

The fact is that most, if not all, ministers could do with help to understand themselves as they move into retirement. In the words of John Weaver, a retired theological college principal, 'The retired person needs support in developing a new stage of self-construction and meaning, for it has been our work or ministry that gives a sense of self-worth, experience, creativity and self-expression, and often an opportunity to serve others.'[44]

For some people retirement also provides an opportunity to rethink and reframe their previous understanding of God. In the words of one retired minister:

> I have found that retirement... has caused me to feel free to ask questions and explore ideas that might challenge some of my previously held beliefs. I have realised, possibly to my regret, that sometimes over the years... I have responded to situations and expressed views that in all honesty were designed more to toe the party line theologically and to say what I knew people wanted to hear, than what was truly in my mind and heart. I find now that while retaining and growing in many of these long-held evangelical beliefs, I have been freed to question and sometimes express doubts that had remained hidden and suppressed over the years.[45]

In such a context an experienced mentor or soul friend can help retired ministers to process their thinking, as they struggle with issues of faith and doubt.

Another way of preparing for retirement is to go on a retreat, exploring what God might be saying at this crucial transition in life. In the same way as Anglican and other ordinands go on retreat just before taking their ordination vows, so perhaps there is a place for ministers going on retreat at the end of their active ministry, preparing themselves for the next stage of the 'journey'.[46]

Even though I have been retired since 2014, as a member of the College of Baptist Ministers I find it helpful to remain accountable for my ongoing 'ministry' in retirement. I have a personal portfolio for 'continuing ministerial development' in which I report on matters relating to applied practice and learning, ministry opportunities, collegiality and spirituality. Then, once a year, I give a written account of my development to four minister friends for their comments.

Paul Stevens, a professor emeritus of marketplace theology and leadership at Regent College, Vancouver, wrote that every retired person needs a small accountability group of people 'who know us well and are willing to meet with us from time to time to examine what we are doing with our lives, with our thoughts, with our talents, and even with our money… They need to explore our vulnerabilities and our strengths, and to name the lie in us.'[47] However, I wonder just how realistic that is for most retired people. Yet all of us, and not least retired ministers, could benefit from a wise mentor or soul friend with whom we talk through the issues facing us. With a life to live and a Lord to serve, we need all the help we can get.

5

Take time to settle down

Plan carefully and you will have plenty; if you act too quickly, you will never have enough.
PROVERBS 21:5 (GNB)

Entering retirement can be challenging for anybody, but it can often be particularly challenging for ministers. More than most people, ministers identify themselves with their work: ministry is their life. Hence, the sense of loss of their role is all the greater. Add to that, as we mentioned earlier, the fact that for most ministers retirement is also marked by the loss of a home, the loss of friends and, where there is substantial downsizing, the loss of possessions and the sense of bereavement is even greater.

Normally when a loved one dies, the bereaved are told that they should make no major decisions within six months, if not a year, of the death. The same principle surely applies to ministerial retirement. Clearly decisions will already have been made with regard to the new home. However, there is much to be said for taking time before making other major decisions.

Here I have in mind, for instance, the question of which church to attend. The nearest church may not always prove to be the best church to join. Take time to explore all the options. In my case, after a year of consideration and heart-searching, I eventually decided to join Chelmsford Cathedral, and what a great experience that has proved to be for me. This experience of what David Adam called 'new territory' has broadened immeasurably my understanding of and approach to worship.[48] I now agree wholeheartedly with David Winter that 'nothing in the week... surpasses the Sunday morning Eucharist... In a new way, heaven opens and I feel absolutely at home.'[49]

Along with making time to choose our new spiritual home, we may profitably take time to explore which new interests to pursue and which forms of service in the wider community to take up. It is unwise to rush in and then later have to withdraw. Nor is it a good idea in the first few months of retirement to lock ourselves into arrangements for looking after the grandchildren. I find it significant that in most Anglican dioceses clergy are not given permission to officiate for the first six months of their retirement. This is to allow for a cooling-off period in which they can adjust to the reality of retirement.

There are good reasons, then, to treat the first year as a decision-free gap year, much of which may well be spent at home, but some of it might be spent travelling. In the course of my interviews, I met one minister and his wife who for the first six months of their gap year toured the country with their caravan. I have known of others who have done a grand tour, visiting friends or relations in such places as North America, New Zealand or Australia. An alternative could perhaps be going overseas to a developing country and working as a volunteer, perhaps with a missionary society or other charity. Clearly finances are limited for most retired ministers and their spouses, but it is amazing what can be achieved with careful planning. Most churches give their retiring minister a small gift; would that these churches could be more generous and imaginative and help their minister (and often hard-working spouse) begin their retirement by exploring a part of the world they have never seen before!

However, whether or not travel is involved, the point I am trying to make is that in that gap year retired ministers are able to take a break, when they can begin to adjust to the many changes which retirement brings. For most ministers it will involve settling into a new home and exploring a new area. Free of commitments, this can be a time for doing something completely different to what they have done before. The fact is that retired ministers need to take their time as they begin to work out the implications of this new stage of their lives.

6

Adopt new virtues

The fruit of the Spirit is love, joy, peace, patience, kindness, generosity, faithfulness, gentleness, and self-control.
GALATIANS 5:22–23

Along with the common Christian virtues mentioned by the apostle Paul in his description of the fruit of the Spirit, new virtues need to be adopted by retired ministers, particularly with regard to their relationship with the local church to which they now belong.

Keith Clements, a former general secretary of the Conference of European Churches, proposed the following virtues for retired ministers:[50]

1 **Thankfulness:** no matter how much or how little we have done, we have all received much more than we have ever been able to give. With the end of full-time ministry of any kind comes the end of the need to prove ourselves. No doubt many times we have preached salvation by grace through faith; now is the time to believe it.

2 **An honest memory:** when tempted to complain about churches and younger ministers today, let's remember what we ourselves were like early in our ministry, and that whatever we may claim to know now, we only gradually learned it, from others and through experience.

3 **A readiness to let go:** we are still called to service, but to serve is not to control. We can and should be available in ways that can be useful in church and society. Retirement brings the privilege of being able to do more of what we really want to do.

4 **A readiness for the new:** retirement is an opportunity for trying something we've never had time, opportunity or even inclination to do before, whether a form of service, study or a leisure activity. You might discover more of the 'you' than you thought was there before.

5 **Discipline:** now that you're 'on your own', free from the programmed routine and demands of church or organisation, it's tempting to think you'll be free of the treadmill of work. However, you may discover that the hardest taskmaster you'll ever have to work for is yourself. Watch out for the signs: becoming at least as busy as you were before.

6 **A large perspective:** 'Nothing worth doing is completed in our lifetime; therefore we must be saved by hope. Nothing true or beautiful makes complete sense in any immediate context of history; therefore we must be saved by faith. Nothing we do, however virtuous, can be accomplished alone; therefore, we are saved by love.'[51]

7 **Capacity to dream:** 'Your old men shall dream dreams, and your young men shall see visions' (Joel 2:28). Retirement should be a time when we're set free to dream again, as in our youth, about the future of the church and the world, even if we not going to be around to see it. Let the imagination run riot and dare to share what you hope for.

Without disagreeing with Keith, I have proposed the following additional virtues:[52]

8 **Wisdom:** to grow in wisdom is to look back on the past and make sense of our lives. Hopefully looking back will create a sense of pride in one's achievements, but it will almost certainly involve coming to terms with disappointment and unfulfilled dreams.

9 **Thankfulness for God's goodness in the past:** ministry has indeed been an amazing privilege, and God has blessed us beyond our deserving. Also thankfulness for the present: instead of grumbling about church life today, we should thank God for the new freedoms that are ours.

10 **Attentiveness:** it is all too easy for retired ministers to talk about themselves and their experience of ministry, rather than lend a listening ear to others who are in one way or another seeking to serve God today.

11 **Encouragement:** ministers need to become angel's advocates, celebrating the achievements of the next generation.

12 **Patience and forbearance:** even when we fundamentally disagree with new ways of doing church, loyalty in ministry requires that we refuse to criticise others, even to our friends.

13 **Steadfastness of faith:** even though we are retired, there is still a race to run and a Lord to serve.

14 **Hope:** let's resist the temptation to be 'sunset' people, looking back, but rather be 'sunrise' people, looking forward to both this life and the life to come.

15 **Love:** let's radiate the love of the Lord Jesus not just to those of our generation, but to the future generations and not least to our own grandchildren, who all too often do not know of God's love for them.

7

Maintain the disciplines

The righteous flourish... In old age they still produce fruit; they are always green and full of sap.
PSALM 92:12, 14

There is a danger in retirement that once the rhythm of sermon preparation and prayerful pastoral care is broken, our formal spiritual disciplines begin to collapse or lose their vibrancy, and as a result our spiritual well-being is affected. If we are to continue to grow and remain fresh in our spirit, then we need to continue to develop our relationship with God. According to Psalm 92, in contrast to 'the wicked' who 'sprout like grass' (v. 7), 'the righteous' flourish like 'the palm tree' and the 'cedar' (v. 12), so that instead of shrivelling up, they 'will still be full of juice in old age'.[53] Artur Weiser commented: 'Amazing energies, which do not let the godly man [*sic*] grow feeble or weak even in old age, are continually imparted to him afresh by his living communion with God.'[54]

This living communion with God is renewed and constantly maintained through the reading of scripture and through prayer. We are to be like the servant of the Lord, of whom the prophet wrote: 'Morning by morning he wakens – wakens my ear to listen as those who are taught' (Isaiah 50:4). As Dietrich Bonhoeffer observed, the time we spend with God at the beginning of the day determines the rest of the day: 'Wasted time, which we are ashamed of, temptations that beset us, weakness and listlessness in our work, disorder and indiscipline in our thinking and our relationships with other people, very frequently have their cause in the neglect of the morning prayer.'[55]

Even in retirement, these simple exercises of devotion require a degree of discipline. But then, discipline is but the other side of discipleship.[56] Or, to put it another way, the disciplines of Bible reading and prayer are our response to the seeking God. In the words of Paul Stevens, these disciplines:

> are not attempts to move God-ward by our own sheer, dogged persistence and effort, pulling ourselves up by our own bootstraps. In fact, we cannot move an inch toward God by our own effort. The reality is that God crosses the infinity of time and space and knocks on our door. And that is what spiritual disciplines do – they are ways of hearing the knocking and opening the door.[57]

There are different ways of maintaining a rule of life. Central to that discipline is the reading of scripture. Some retired ministers use daily Bible reading notes, while others create their own system of reading through books of the Bible, either with or without a commentary.[58] For many years, as part of my discipline, I have found using the Anglican *Revised Common Lectionary* helpful. It provides me with a rich, varied diet of scripture, with readings drawn every day from the Old and New Testaments. It also enables me to pray daily through the Psalms. As I read, whenever a phrase or a verse jumps out at me, I mark my Bible and then, for a shorter or longer period, I try to 'chew' over what God may be saying to me.

Retirement is a time for a fresh encounter with God. In the words of Cuthbert Bardsley, a former bishop of Coventry:

> It is important to take time in our old age to be still, so that we can become more aware of the God who makes Himself known in the quietness… In the prayer of old age we shall learn to float on the all-pervasive, all-available strength and love of God. We shall learn to relax and to listen to the still small voice of God.[59]

Growing old, with the pressures of time removed, is in fact a great opportunity for drawing nearer to God. 'Indeed,' said H.P. Steer, 'that may well be its main purpose: and each day becomes a day of opportunity, a day of spiritual growth, of radiating, albeit unconsciously, something of the peace and power of God to others.'[60]

8

Delight in a changing relationship

The Lord God said, 'It is not good that the man should be alone; I will make him a helper as his partner.'
GENESIS 2:18

For ministers who are married, retirement is an opportunity to delight in a changing relationship with our life-partners. At our golden wedding celebration, I quoted an article from *Good Housekeeping* giving tips for 'staying together power'.[61] These included:

1 Talk to each other, don't vent to friends.
2 Never stop creating shared memories: do things together.
3 Kids make marriage stronger.
4 Give each other personal space.
5 Marriage is not always 50/50.
6 Embrace your individuality: it's important to be your own person.
7 Don't overlook small family moments.
8 Love means being a team when problems arise.
9 Never stop showing affection.
10 Have a standing date – without the kids.

I dare to think our marriage, with its changing patterns of relationships, has reflected some of those tips. Precisely how things will work out once we are both retired is unclear. However, one thing is clear: we will ensure that we have time to do things together – but also time to do things as individuals. We both need our own space!

As for how other retired ministers with spouses experience retirement, I discovered that some spouses found the transition difficult. For instance, 'it has been difficult fitting into church life – change of roles'; 'she misses people very much and can feel lonely'; 'it has not been easy having to uproot once more and set up new relationships – but she is very resilient'; 'she has found it more difficult than I have leaving some very close friends in our last church and feeling quite unhappy here with issues with the house, etc. She is more content now and is finding a few roles in the church'. On the other hand, some spouses appreciated the transition. For instance, 'she is pleased to be free from church "politics"'; 'she is able to have meaningful friendships more than when I was a minister'; 'she now appreciates the possibility of being an "ordinary" member of the church and not having to live up to people's expectations'; 'instead of duties she now has choices'. For a few spouses, retirement has entailed fresh opportunities: one, for instance, 'has taken on spiritual direction and runs the diocese training course for new spiritual directors'; another is 'seeking to re-establish opportunities to continue her piano tuition in a new area'.[62]

In response to the question 'How has retirement affected your relationship with your spouse?', some retired ministers said not much had changed. 'Our relationship,' replied one minister, 'is as strong as before.' For others, retirement appears to have enhanced relationships: 'we have grown closer together, become more interdependent, but have also lost some individual independence'; 'we pray together more, we sit in church together'; 'we have more time together – especially evenings'; 'we have more time to do things together – we have taken the opportunity to foster involvement in activities outside the church and we also appreciate having weekends to visit family and friends'.[63]

The important thing is to be positive and to recognise that retirement is an opportunity to 'rebuild the fire' and to delight in our changing relationship. In the words of John Powell:

We are standing within arm's reach of that which is most humanly rewarding and beautiful. We must not turn back now. We can still share all the things we once shared with such excitement, when first I told you who I was and you told me who you were; only now our sharing will be deeper because we are deeper.

If I will continue to hear you with the same sense of wonder and joy as I did in the beginning, and you will hear me in this way, our friendship will grow firmer and deeper roots. The tinsel of our first sharing will mellow into gold. We can be sure that there is no need to hide anything from each other, since we have shared everything.[64]

II

Finding new purpose

9

Be secure in your real identity

The Son of God... loved me and gave himself for me.
GALATIANS 2:20

Baptist minister John Rackley, in a retreat address entitled 'Will you still love me when I'm 64?', reflected on how the 'heart that he gave to the Lord Jesus Christ' at the age of seven was now very different at the age of 64. He said, 'God asks, "What is it about me that still captivates you? What is it about me that still holds you?" If God were an Ignatian, the question would be "What is your image of me?"'[65]

As I reflect on those two questions, my first answer is: I am captivated by the love of God 'for me'. Every time I eat bread and drink wine at the Lord's table, I am overwhelmed afresh by the love of Jesus 'for me'. Not for nothing did Martin Luther say, 'Meditate well on these little words ME and for ME.' Here we see the wonder of the love of Jesus for each one of us. In the words of a hymn penned by Charles Wesley (1707–88) just a day or two after his heart was 'strangely warmed':

And can it be that I should gain
An interest in the Saviour's blood?
Died he for me, who caused his pain?
For me, who him to death pursued?
Amazing love! How can it be
That thou, my God, shouldst die for me!

My image of God is related to the massive sculpture of 'Christ in Glory' suspended high over the nave of Chelmsford Cathedral: the arms of the risen Christ are outstretched in welcome, while his hands and feet still carry the scars of the cross. Every time I go forward to receive the bread and wine I look up at this wonderful figure, and as I do so my mind goes to 'Just as I am', a hymn which in many evangelical circles today is often associated with conversion, but which was originally written by Charlotte Elliott (1789–1871) as a hymn of consecration. This in turn makes it a very appropriate hymn for Communion:[66]

Just as I am; you will receive,
Will welcome, pardon, cleanse, relieve;
Because your promise I believe,
O Lamb of God, I come.

Just as I am; your love unknown
Has broken every barrier down:
Now to be yours, yes yours alone
O Lamb of God, I come.

Here is my ultimate identity: in spite of all my failings and imperfections, the crucified, risen and ascended Jesus loves me and I am his forever. This is what captivates me. This is what motivates me. I am loved by God. Here I find my security – in both this life and the next. In the final chapter of *This is My Story*, I wrote: 'As I look back over my life, there is so much for which I am grateful – and for which I thank God.' Of the eight reasons which I identified for gratitude the very first was: 'I thank God for his amazing love for me seen above all in Jesus. What a difference Jesus makes to living (and, of course, to dying too).'[67]

All too often, one of the first questions we ask of people we meet is 'What do you do?', as if what really counts is a person's role in life. But ultimately our identity has nothing to do with what we do (or what we have done), but rather with who we are. For me that identity is found in the love of Jesus for me. 'I am my beloved's and my beloved is mine' (Song of Songs 6:3). Or, in the words of the hymn by Frances van Alstyne (1820–1915),[68] to which the title of my autobiography alludes:

Blessed assurance Jesus is mine:
O what a foretaste of glory divine!
Heir of salvation, purchase of God;
Born of his Spirit, washed in his blood.

This is my story, this is my song,
Praising my Saviour all the day long.

To some this may all sound very simple. But then, the great theologian Karl Barth, after a lecture at the University of Chicago in 1926, is said to have summed up his theology in the simple lines of a children's chorus by Anna Bartlett Warner (1827–1915):

Jesus loves me! this I know,
For the Bible tells me so.

For many ministers, retirement undermines our sense of identity. Previously our identity was defined by our job, but with retirement everything changes and there is no longer a role or status that belongs to us. But the reality is that our security is not found in ourselves, but in Jesus and his love for us.

In this regard I am reminded of how the Archbishop of Canterbury Justin Welby responded to the surprising discovery that his biological father was not Gavin Welby, but rather Sir Anthony Montague Brown. For many people, their sense of identity is bound up with their roots. However, Justin Welby issued a statement in which he said, 'I know that I find who I am in Jesus Christ, not in genetics, and my identity in him never changes.' He went on to speak of 'the grace and power of Christ to liberate and redeem us, grace and power which is offered to every human being' and ended with an account of his inauguration service three years previously, when Evangeline Kanagasooriam, a young member of the Canterbury Cathedral congregation, said, 'We greet you in the name of Christ. Who are you, and why do you request entry?' Justin Welby replied, 'I am Justin, a servant of Jesus Christ, and I come as one seeking the grace of God to travel with you in his service together.'

The challenge here is for each one of us to find our true identity in Christ, however we might express it.

10

Live out your call

God… set me apart before I was born and called me through his grace.
GALATIANS 1:15

Most retired ministers believe that God still has a call on their life. Retirement is not the end of ministry. Significantly the document containing the Church of England's advice to Anglican dioceses on how they should care for their retired clergy is headed, 'Supporting the ministry of retired clergy'.[69] In the report's foreword, the bishop of Manchester, David Walker, wrote:

Ordination to the Priesthood, in the Church of England, is understood as a life-long vocation… Ordained ministers are called, without any limit of time, as long as they live, to proclaim the glory of God in every part of their lives, not just in the exercise of celebrating public services.[70]

Although Baptists have a different approach to ordination and do not talk of ministry in terms of priesthood, nonetheless in recent years they have adopted an increasingly sacramental, as distinct from a functional, approach to ministry, in which ministry is viewed effectively as an 'indelible act' from which there can be no turning back: once a minister, then a minister forever.[71] Thus in my survey of retired Baptist ministers, 81% of respondents declared: 'Ordination is for life, so God continues to have a call on my life.' Paul Goodliff, writing in his former capacity of ministries team leader of the Baptist Union of Great Britain, expressed this sense of call as follows:

If ministry at its heart is the offering of a life of discipleship in the service of Christ, his church and his world, do we ever 'retire'? At the very least much of what has been the focus of our way of life will continue in a different shape, tenor and key... prayerfulness, service, witness, care for others. This is the stuff of the common experience of discipleship, and ministers (we hope) do not cease from being followers of Jesus because they no longer draw a stipend... Retirement signifies a greater freedom of choice in how we use our time and talents, while remaining subject to the 'long obedience in the same direction' that is the common experience of all who live under the rule of Christ. It reflects, probably, a laying down of the demands of oversight, pastoral charge of a congregation and much of the profound sense of responsibility only ever really understood by those to whom is committed the charge of a congregation of God's people... One hopes that the sometimes frenetic pace of life that stipendiary ministry... demands will be replaced by a more sedate, and probably healthier, way of life, with more time for family and friends and opportunities to renew old interests and discover new pursuits. All of this is part of the rich pathway of discipleship and ministry.[72]

I like the description of Christian discipleship as a 'long obedience in the same direction', which in this context is almost certainly an allusion to Eugene Peterson's book of the same title,[73] which interestingly is itself taken from some perceptive words of Friedrich Nietzsche:

The essential thing 'in heaven and earth' is... that there should be long obedience in the same direction; there thereby results, and has always resulted in the long run, something which has made life worth living.[74]

Louis Armstrong, the great jazz musician, once said, 'Musicians don't retire; they stop when there's no more music in them.' That too is how most of us retired ministers feel: we still have divine music in our souls, and we will only stop giving voice to that music when we join the greater chorus in heaven.[75]

However, it is important for retired ministers to realise that we are no longer pastors. We no longer have a church to run and should let go of any desire to do so. Retirement is about letting go and entrusting the church to the Lord of the church. In this regard I found the following comment from an Anglican perspective most helpful: 'Priests never retire, but vicars do… They relinquish jobs, but not their vocations.'[76] Although Baptists do not normally refer to their ministers as 'priests', I find the use of this term here unusually meaningful. A priest by definition is a 'bridge' between God and the world; the Latin word for priest (*pontifex*) literally means 'bridge-builder'. I believe that part of my ongoing calling has a 'priestly' aspect to it: in all that I am and do, I am called to serve as a 'bridge' between God and others.

Precisely how we live out our calling will vary from person to person, and will vary, too, according to our health and strength. What retired ministers have in common is that we are free to serve God in new ways and 'on our own terms' – without the expectations and pressures of church people.[77]

Many retired ministers are busily involved in serving God in his church. In my survey of retired Baptist ministers, 85% continued to preach and lead Bible studies; 55% continued to take funerals from time to time; 47% helped with pastoral care; 36% led a home or small group; and 21% mentored younger ministers.[78]

Along with many other retired ministers of my age, I am still keen to use my experience and energy in the service of God. For me one important way of living out my call and serving God has been devoting time to writing. I write not because I have any pretensions to literary ability, but because others have recognised that I have the gift of expressing the complex in a simple and logical way. Since standing down from stipendiary ministry, I have written a number of books. Another key aspect of my current ministry is writing Church

Matters, a weekly blog which I started in autumn 2011. Every week I receive responses from all over the world: it is almost like having a virtual congregation, except that the blogs take the place of sermons. In addition, I have also sought to live out my call in retirement by engaging in further ministry research. Hence in spring 2017 I sent out questionnaires to almost 2,000 Baptist ministers about their reading habits: over 300 ministers responded and the results were published in an 8,000-word article in the *Baptist Quarterly*.[79] Then, as I have mentioned already in the introduction, in 2018 I embarked on another research project to see how ministers experience retirement, which resulted in my report, *Retirement Matters for Ministers*. In 2019, on the basis of a further research project focused on the experience of Baptist ministers who in their retirement worship in Anglican churches, I wrote *Entering New Territory*.

This ministry of writing and research is one way in which I seek to live out my calling. Other retired ministers no doubt live out their calling in other ways, whether through engagement in their local church or in service in the wider world beyond the church. There is no one pattern for ministry in retirement. What is important is that in one way or another we seek to be faithful to the call that God has on our lives.

11

Don't just hand out the hymn books

We have gifts that differ according to the grace given to us.
ROMANS 12:6

I belong to Chelmsford Cathedral not because Baptist principles no longer matter to me, but because I wanted to be part of a larger church, where I felt I could be freer to serve God in my own way. I am now part of the clergy team which leads the Sunday 'Breakfast with the Bible', a presentation-led weekly series of Bible studies. I also lead and host one of the home 'fellowship' groups. But I do not hand out the hymn books; nor do I help take up the collection; nor am I part of the cathedral's welcome team. I have been tempted to join the team responsible for the intercessions and the team responsible for serving the wine at the weekly Eucharist, but I have resisted these 'temptations'. I have 'done my time', so it is best to give younger people the opportunity for those forms of service.

Filling the time is for most retired ministers not a problem. The challenge is to become involved in activities that enrich and satisfy us. In this regard, looking at some of the responses in my survey of how Baptist ministers experience retirement, I was surprised to see so many were engaged in what I would regard as simply helping to run their local church. For example, many were involved in groups tasked with planning worship or running Alpha; exercising pastoral care or devising church publicity; others were involved in running a church bookstall or editing a church newsletter; playing the piano for services; serving as a church cleaner; or being part of a church maintenance team. Of course, if we believe that this is what God wants us to do to live out our calling, then clearly it is right to do so. However, at times I felt that some of my fellow retired ministers were responding to needs, rather than serving according to their gifting. (Having said that, if needs are not being met by others and we are able to help, then that is a good reason to do so.) As the apostle Paul reminds us, 'we have gifts that differ' (Romans 12:6), and he wants people to use their particular gifts. For me, retirement means being free of the routine tasks of church life; having spent a lifetime in such service, I now want to focus on what I perceive to be my calling in my retirement.

Furthermore, our calling as retired ministers should surely not just be restricted to service in the church. There is a much bigger world beyond the church, where we are called to be salt and light (Matthew 5:13–16). The kingdom is bigger than the church. In that respect I was delighted to see that 40% of respondents in my research on retirement said that they worked as volunteers in the community.[80]

The question arises: are these forms of service essentially leisure activities – or something more? Some believe that in the early years of retirement each of us needs consciously to develop a second career, which is quite different from a leisure activity. These second careers, wrote Paul Tournier, take precedence over more selfish pleasures and demand that we create a mission statement for ourselves with clearly defined goals. He went on to say that such careers 'will have no age-limit, no routine, no fixed wage tied to an obligation to work. It can be voluntary, it can be paid, but without any compulsory relationship between earnings and output. It has nothing, therefore, to do with the idea of a second *job*'.[81]

Although I can understand the desire of many to give meaning to their retirement by discovering new avenues of service in the community, I am not convinced that ministers who have devoted a lifetime to serving others need to find another formal expression of service in their retirement. For me, one of the joys of retirement from pastoring a local church is the freedom to discover new and changing ways of serving God and others. Yet so much depends on our circumstances, and not least the age when we retire. Had I retired at the age of 60, for instance, the idea of a second career in local politics might well have appealed to me. As it was, I retired at the age of 70 and therefore gave the idea little further consideration.

The issue, however, is that whatever we do, we think about giving meaning and shape to the way in which we spend our active retirement, and so discover satisfaction and fulfilment in our service to God and to others.

12

Keep your mind fresh

Iron sharpens iron, and one person sharpens the wits of another.
PROVERBS 27:17

'There are worse crimes than burning books,' said the Russian-American poet Joseph Brodsky. 'One of them is not reading them.'[82] As a working minister I used to say, 'A book a week keeps a pastor awake.' Retired ministers too need to keep awake. Maybe for some a book a week is too demanding: but whether it is a book a week, a fortnight or even just a month, we need to keep our minds fresh, with a book always on the go.

Reading is vital if we are to keep spiritually and intellectually fresh. The danger is that if we are always giving out and never getting any input, we soon have little to offer and become just loquacious bores.[83]

I am in the fortunate position of receiving a constant flow of books, two or three a week, to review for my blog, Church Matters. For other retired ministers looking for inspiration as to what to read, let me commend my blog; every other month I post a host of book reviews under the heading 'Books for today'. To help people know what to buy I always recommend a book of the month. Recent books of the month have included *Praying Psalms: A personal journey through the psalter* by Ian Stackhouse; *Everything Happens for a Reason and Other Lies I've Loved* by Kate Bowler; *Phoebe* by Paula Gooder; *Sinners and Saints: The real story of Christianity* by Derek Cooper;

Praying the Way with Matthew, Mark, Luke and John by Terry Hinks; and *Following Jesus in Turbulent Times: Disciple-making in the Arab world* by Hikmat Kashouh.

However, we don't have to keep on buying new books in order to keep our minds fresh. I would imagine that most of us have on our shelves books we never got round to reading, and there also may well be books we could profitably reread. Indeed, C.S. Lewis maintained that 'it is a good rule after reading a new book, never to allow yourself another new one till you have read an old one in between. If that is too much for you, you should read one old one to every three new ones.'[84]

There are other ways of growing and developing too, apart from just reading. Lifelong learning need not be a solitary discipline. There is much to be said for learning together. It is as we interact with others, sharing and debating ideas, that we become more alive and interesting as people. 'Iron sharpens iron, and one person sharpens the wits of another,' says Proverbs 27:17. Meetings for retired ministers can involve more than simply fellowship – they can also involve theological reflection and stimulation. Another possibility is to join a theological society or a study group. Most Anglican dioceses have a theological society to which ministers of other denominations are welcome.

Another way is to develop new learning skills. One acquaintance of mine taught himself classical Greek and read all of Homer in his retirement. As a minister, whenever I visited the recently retired, I would encourage them not just to find new ways of serving the church, but also to find new ways of developing their minds. 'What about learning Japanese?' I would sometimes suggest. Alternatively, another possibility would be to freshen up old skills. I confess that in my own case, in recent years the modern languages which I studied at Cambridge have become somewhat rusty, with the result that I have decided to begin to read some novels in French and German.

Yet another way of keeping the mind fresh is to read again some of the texts studied at school, for which we did not then have the maturity to truly appreciate their content. In my first year at secondary school I had to read John Bunyan's *The Pilgrim's Progress*, but at the time I failed to make much sense of it, let alone to enjoy it. Similarly in sixth form, when I was studying Greek and Latin, I read some of the great books of classical literature, but as a teenager without any real experience of life I failed to appreciate much of what I read; now, a lifetime later, is a good time to revisit these texts from my past.

'The glory of God is a human being fully alive,' Irenaeus is reputed to have said.[85] To be fully alive we need to be all that we can be, living life to the full by using our heart and our mind, our soul and our strength, to discover more and more the goodness of God's creation.

13

Become a sage

Let the wise also hear and gain in learning, and the discerning acquire skill.
PROVERBS 1:5

There is more to ageing than simply growing older. It is true that some wines improve with age, but that is only if the grapes were good in the first place! We need to grow in wisdom. Wisdom is not an automatic gift; it is something which is developed through reflection upon experience. In this respect Zalman Schachter-Shalomi, a Jewish commentator, helpfully wrote:

> One is only old by the calendar, but one becomes an elder when one knows how to use those years, and that means life review, life repair, relationship repair, and a way of thinking about, how do I want to harvest what I learned in life. And there are good memories and there are some other memories that are not so happy, but they contain in themselves some good too, if one looks into them.[86]

Part of that life review involves learning from past failures and becoming wiser as a result. Indeed, according to the American Franciscan Richard Rohr, in his aptly termed book *Falling Upward*, the pathway to spiritual maturity only comes through failure: 'Those who have gone "down" are the only ones who understand "up".'[87] He went on:

> The bottom line of the Gospel is that most of us have to hit some kind of bottom before we even start the spiritual journey... so do not waste a moment of time lamenting poor parenting, lost job, failed relationship, physical handicap, gender identity, economic poverty, or even the tragedy of any kind of abuse. Pain is part of the deal.[88]

It is a sobering thought that wisdom does not emerge from 'success', but rather from the crucible of pain and loss. As I know from my own personal experience, trials are to be welcomed (James 1:2–4), for the truth is that 'all sunshine makes a desert'.

Becoming a sage involves looking back on our past and making sense of our lives. Hopefully, such looking back will create a sense of pride as one perhaps becomes aware of one's true achievements. Almost certainly, looking back will also involve coming to terms with disappointment; the fact is that for most of us there will be unfulfilled dreams.

Becoming a sage involves a good deal of self-awareness. Yet few of us are truly self-aware. To make sense of our past and of ourselves we often need others – spiritual directors, soul friends, therapists – so we can begin to share the wisdom drawn from their experience of life.

It is only as retired ministers 'wise up' that they can be mentors. I find it interesting that the word 'mentor' comes from a character in Homer's classic epic poem *Odyssey*, where Mentor, an old and trusted friend of Odysseus, was left behind as the warriors embarked for Troy, to keep an eye on Odysseus' household and in particular to be a wise counsellor to Telemachus, the headstrong but sometimes wavering son of Odysseus. Mentor linked the wisdom of the past to the uncertainties of the future.

The Bible, too, provides examples of mentoring relationships: Jethro and Moses; Moses and Joshua; Naomi and Ruth; Eli and

Samuel; Barnabas and Paul; Paul and his team of helpers (especially Timothy); and above all, Jesus and the twelve. However, probably the truly foundational passage on mentoring in the Bible is found in Proverbs 1—9, where the 'teacher' uses his knowledge and experience to provide direction for the 'learner'. Daniel Estes commented: 'The ultimate goal… is that the learner will develop independent competence in living responsibly in Yahweh's world… The teacher is at times an expert, at times a facilitator, but always the guide, pointing the learners toward their own independent competence.'[89]

Sometimes, however, the role we can play is just to be there, to serve as a listening ear, as a minister, perhaps, pours out his or her heart. Paul Tournier recommended that instead of giving advice, 'the old have something better to do – to become confidants. We will open our hearts to those who will listen to understand us, and not in order to judge or direct us.'[90]

14

Encourage your minister

Encourage one another and build up each other.
1 THESSALONIANS 5:11

There is one ministry in which I would urge every retired minister to be involved: the ministry of encouragement, and in particular the ministry of encouraging the minister(s) of the church.[91] According to William James, 'The deepest principle in human nature is the craving to be appreciated.'[92] Although all God's people need encouragement (see, for instance, Hebrews 10:25), this is particularly true of ministers. Ministry can be tough. There are good times, but there can be challenging times too. What a difference it made to us when, after we had given our all, a member of the congregation came up and expressed a word of encouragement.

I shall never forget my first experience of Spring Harvest, the Easter holiday Bible teaching event. At the very first meeting of speakers and helpers, one of the leaders challenged us to major on the positive. Instead of being critical, he asked us to find something positive to say about the sessions. Amazingly, this was what happened. It became a truly affirming experience for us all.

The Greek verb normally translated by our English word 'encourage' (*parakaleo*) literally means 'to come alongside'. It can have the sense of 'to instil someone with courage or cheer', and the cognate noun (*paraclete*) is used by John of the Holy Spirit in the farewell discourses of Jesus (John 14—16). When we as retired ministers draw alongside those in active ministry with a word of encouragement, are we actually sharing in the ministry of God himself?

I know from my own experience as a minister that the tendency of so many church members is to criticise rather than to praise, and in this context how much a word of encouragement meant to me. So I now make it my business to thank the preacher of the day for the sermon, and I will often follow up the comment with an email reflecting on the sermon or on some aspect of the worship. Further, in my conversations with congregational members at the after-service coffee, I regularly express my appreciation for the ministry of the church. Incidentally, sometimes actions can helpfully accompany words: so take your minister out for a coffee, and when you have a party include your minister and his or her spouse!

In turn the clergy team is amazingly welcoming of me. This is amazing not least because theologically we come from different 'stables'. However, I make a conscious effort not to criticise but to affirm. As a result, I have been blessed with good relationships with the members of the ministerial team of the church I now attend.

By contrast, in my survey of how ministers experience retirement, I discovered that a third of those responding did not have a positive relationship with the minister of their church and that only around two-fifths said they would 'count the minister as a friend'.[93] I wonder if relationships might have improved if there had been more encouragement.

The encouragement of our successors in active ministry needs to become a regular discipline for retired ministers. We need to become angel's advocates, always looking for what is good and then supporting it. 'You may be surprised how much good there is to find!'[94]

15

Keep looking to Jesus

Let us run with perseverance the race that is set before us, looking to Jesus.
HEBREWS 12:1–2

I am not sure when for me the race first began. In one sense I began the race when I was baptised as a believer at the age of 14 on Sunday 17 November 1957, just a stone's throw from the river Limmat, where the Swiss reformer Ulrich Zwingli had drowned Anabaptist women. Or did the race begin the Sunday evening when, at the age of 8, I knelt down and asked Jesus to come into my heart to be my Saviour and my Lord? But in the context of ministry, it was at the age of 25, when I was ordained, that the race began. And here I am now in the stadium – soon to finish the race.

Over the years, for some of us, the youthful commitment to Jesus tends to wane. The older we grow, sometimes the flabbier we become, not just physically but also spiritually. We become cynical and half-hearted, and begin to go through the motions of religion. Or at least, that is the danger. Sadly, for some, ministry becomes just a job. In retirement the temptation for us is to freewheel rather than continue to pull out all the stops as we go the way of Jesus. Physically we may be running down, but retirement is no excuse for decadence.[95]

The apostle Paul also took up the metaphor of the Christian life as a race. Writing to the church at Philippi, Paul spoke of his personal determination to 'press on towards the goal for the prize of the heavenly call of God in Christ Jesus' (Philippians 3:14; see also v. 12). This involved on the one hand 'forgetting what lies behind'; the context suggests that Paul had in mind not past failures but past achievements. On the other hand, it involved 'straining forward to what lies ahead' (v. 13). Even after many years of Christian service Paul was not tempted to take life a little easier and perhaps enjoy the good things of life (see v. 19). He gave the race everything he had: 'in those words the lungs burn, the temples pound, the muscles ache, the heart pumps, the perspiration rolls'.[96] Even in the very closing stages of his life Paul was conscious that the race was not over: the bell may have sounded for the final lap, but he had yet to go through the tape. For although Paul says he had 'fought the good fight' and had 'finished the race' (2 Timothy 4:7), he used a Greek perfect tense, which implies a past action which continues into the present.

The marathon race in which we are engaged is not yet over. On those days when we feel as if we are flagging, the writer to the Hebrews encourage us to 'run… looking to Jesus' (Hebrews 12:2). The GNB translates: 'Let us keep our eyes fixed on Jesus.' A better translation is 'looking alone to Jesus' – or rather, 'looking away from other things' we are to 'look to Jesus'.[97] As Peter T. O'Brien said, 'The author's appeal calls for concentrated attention that turns away from all distractions with eyes only for Jesus.'[98] He went on: 'The verb occurs in the description of the Maccabean martyrs who "avenged their nation, looking to God, and enduring the torments to the point of death" (4 Maccabees).'[99]

Focused concentration on Jesus is what is in mind. It is what William Lane called 'contemplation of Jesus'.[100] I am reminded of the Roman Catholic custom of the adoration of 'the host', that is, the consecrated elements used in the Mass. If you go into a Roman Catholic cathedral, you will see people kneeling before the altar and staying there on their knees, adoring the host. As Protestants we may not adore the host, but we too must learn to adore the Saviour, to focus on him, to concentrate on him.

In this regard, William Lane pointed out that in Hebrews 12 we are not called to focus on the Saviour, nor on the Lord, nor on the Christ, nor indeed on the Son of God, but on 'Jesus': 'The use of the simple personal name "Jesus" shows that the accent is upon his humanity, and especially his endurance of pain, humiliation and the disgrace of the cross.'[101] Jesus, in the very way in which he lived life God's way, has set us a pattern for our living. We need to keep on looking to him, and in looking begin to imitate his life.

III

Living a full life

16

Relax and play

I came that they may have life, and have it abundantly.
JOHN 10:10

The Bible speaks a good deal about the sabbath. Rest and relaxation are part of God's pattern for our living. For instance, 'In six days the Lord made heaven and earth, and on the seventh day he rested, and was refreshed' (Exodus 31:17). The Hebrew word translated here 'rested' means literally 'took a deep breath'. The context of this verse is keeping the sabbath: the implication is that if God needed to take a deep breath after all his hard work in creation, then surely all the more we need to do the same and balance work with rest. As Claire Foster, the co-founder of St Paul's Institute for Ethics in Finance and Business, has pointed out:

There is nothing that works against a lifestyle that cares about creation more than being in a hurry. Too much of a hurry to ponder shopping choices. Too much of a hurry to walk rather than drive. Too much of a hurry to cook. Too much of a hurry to grow food. Too much of a hurry to turn off the TV and play with our children or grandchildren. Too much of a hurry to sleep properly and give the world a rest from our self-important busyness. Finally, perhaps, too much of a hurry to have noticed the damage we have done to the planet, before it is too late. We need to step back and take the time to look, to learn about what we see, so that we can appreciate in more and more astonishing detail the beauty of what we see, and we can love it, if we but give ourselves the time.[102]

Then there is the 'great invitation' of Jesus: 'Come to me, all you that are weary and are carrying heavy burdens, and I will give you rest' (Matthew 11:28). Or in the version used by the *Book of Common Prayer* of the Church of England, read at every 1662 communion service as one of the 'comfortable words': 'Come unto me, all ye that travail and are heavy-laden, and I will refresh you.' These are words which are particularly appropriate to ministry, for Jesus was talking in the first place to those who had been worn out by religion. Eugene Peterson in his paraphrase Bible, *The Message*, has Jesus say: 'Are you tired? Worn out? Burned out on religion? Come to me. Get away with me and you'll recover your life.'

After a lifetime of working long hours in the service of God, by the time we retire many ministers are well and truly worn out. We need time to recover. We need time for 'R and R'. What's more, as our years increase, the energy levels of most of us begin to decrease, with the result that we cannot keep up with the pace we once set ourselves.

Retirement offers an opportunity for rest and relaxation. David Winter helpfully called retirement 'the "sabbath" of life; the evening's rest awaiting us at the end of a lifetime of work and responsibility'.[103] 'Relax,' he wrote. 'Take your foot off the gas. There's no need now to live life in the fast lane. There's time to do things, to think, to make plans. Don't rush it! Space and time are gifts of God – use them.'[104] As James Woodward put it, 'Growing older is about adding life to years rather than just adding years to our lives.'[105]

Retirement is an opportunity for play. For some modern-day puritans, this concept of play is hard to justify. However, it is significant that the prophets Isaiah and Zechariah envisioned the kingdom of God, God's shalom, as a time when infants and children would be playing with no fear (Isaiah 11:6–8; Zechariah 8:4–5). Jaco Hamman commented: 'In these images we can recognise Jesus inviting children to come to him, for the kingdom of heaven belongs to children and those like them. We hear Jesus offering to all life to the full, which certainly is not possible without the transformative power of play (Matthew 19:14; John 10:10b).'[106] 'Playing,' Hamman said, 'can help us "toy" with, and discover, God's shalom.'[107]

By contrast, some recent Christian writers take issue with the whole concept of retirement and relaxation. Rodney Macready, an Australian, in his book *Retiring Retirement* argued that Christians should not retire.[108] He wrote: 'If you're already retired and in the middle of a self-indulgent binge, I want you to repent. You may think you're entitled to this – that it's your God-given right after years of hard work. I don't think you'll find that in the Bible.'[109] Much of the book is given up to detailed biblical exegesis, seeking to prove that we have been created to work, and that the biblical ideal for the aged was 'much more active, engaged and responsible for the community than the modern practice of retirement encourages us to be'.[110]

I confess that much of the author's careful engagement with scripture left me cold – it just seemed totally irrelevant. As I read about the Levites in Numbers 8 or the widows in 1 Timothy 5, I said to myself, 'So what?' Life in the ancient world was so totally different that I am not convinced that the principles which the author seeks to apply to our world today are hermeneutically sound. True, I agree with Macready that some retired Christians can be amazingly self-indulgent. However, self-indulgence is hard to define. I am not convinced, for instance, that 'enjoying a luxury cruise' or 'taking an extended holiday' are good examples of self-indulgence. On the other hand, I do question whether spending day after day playing golf or bridge is the right use of time for a Christian. I recognise, however, that my judgement could be impaired insofar as I do not enjoy playing golf or bridge, but I do appreciate holidays. Whatever the case, my point is that there is a rightful place for relaxation and play, not least in retirement. On the other hand, there is more to retirement than just relaxation or play. God still has a claim on our lives even as retired people. As the apostle Paul wrote: 'Be careful how you live... Make good use of every opportunity you have' (Ephesians 5:15–16, GNB).

As retired ministers, we are free agents, free to choose what we do. Instead of being accountable to others every day, we are now accountable only to God. That is wonderfully liberating. We are free to rest, and yet God still has a call on our lives. Many of us are not ready for a rocking chair. Richard Morgan spoke of Caleb, who 'asked for a challenge, not a cushion' (see Joshua 14:10–12), who 'wanted more adventures in his "retirement years"'. Yet Morgan wrote of the need for 'balance between vital involvement and quiet solitude'. He ended with a thought-provoking quotation from Father Donald X: 'The brevity of my life dictates that I must not waste it. At the same time I must not take it too seriously. I must not grasp at it as though it were indeed the "end all and be all" of my existence.'[111]

So we can conclude that there is a place for play, for travel, for adventure. This is the time to pursue new interests, to develop new hobbies, to enjoy the world of music and of art. This is God's world, and as his children we have every right to delight in his creation. But there is also a race to be won, a fight to be fought, a cross to bear – even in retirement.

17

Keep fit and walk

Health and fitness are better than any gold, and a robust body than countless riches.
SIRACH 30:15

Keeping fit is vital. Studies reveal that low levels of increased activity can make a huge difference – 30 minutes of moderately intense exercise five times a week can reduce the risk of developing heart diseases, strokes, type-2 diabetes, some cancers and even dementia.[112] From a rational perspective, exercise is therefore not an option.

I have never been sporty: I only played rugby for the school second XV. But I have always enjoyed walking. In retirement I walk three or so miles with a friend twice a week at seven o'clock in the morning, and in addition I often walk by myself once or twice a week. It's all about trying to keep fit. Of course, walking is not the only form of exercise open to us: we can swim, go the gym and play sport. However, for older people walking is the easiest, and perhaps safest, form of exercise – and it's free! Hence, the encouragement often given is for us to walk 10,000 steps a day.

We have heard much about obesity among children. However, I had not realised that rates for older people are also concerning. According to the 2014 Health Survey for England, the following groups of older people are obese or overweight: 78% of men aged 65–74; 80% of men aged 75–84; and over 70% of women aged 65–84.

I have no statistics for retired ministers, but I did discover that a 2001 Pulpit and Pew study of 2,500 American clergy found that 76% were overweight or obese compared to 61% of the general population at the time of the study. In 2010 Erik Raymond blogged: 'One thing that has always intrigued me is overweight pastors. If you want to get a gauge on how prevalent this is, you just have to visit a pastors' conference. I am not saying that everyone is rockin' the elastic waist pants, but there are a lot of guys that, well, are fat.'[113] Another piece of American research has also shown that ministers tend to be fatter than their church members, and that churchgoers tend to be fatter than non-churchgoers.[114] Although I have no statistics for the UK, my observation is that there are a good number of obese ministers around.

To combat this obesity epidemic, we need – if we are able – to walk. According to Age UK:

- Walking helps with weight loss by burning off calories.
- Brisk walking reduces the risk of coronary heart disease.
- Walking reduces the risk of developing cancer.
- Walking reduces the risk of developing type-2 diabetes.
- Walking strengthens our bones and so helps prevent osteoporosis.
- Walking improves our mind and mental well-being and can even help relieve depression.
- Walking reduces the risk of developing dementia.[115]

Walking certainly appears to be the favourite form of exercise for retired ministers: around one-third (36%) regularly take long walks, while another third (34%) take either 'moderate' or 'occasional' walks. However, exercise of any kind, whether it is bowls or golf, cycling or swimming or even skiing, is good.[116]

If our bodies are temples of the Holy Spirit (1 Corinthians 6:19), then there is no place for abusing them. To counter all the good food and drink that comes our way, perhaps we should get into the routine of walking! As the 19th-century politician Edward Stanley said, 'Those who think they have no time for bodily exercise will sooner or later have to find time for illness.'[117] Or in the words of Jesus son of Sirach, 'Better off poor, healthy, and fit than rich and afflicted in body. Health and fitness are better than any gold, and a robust body than countless riches' (Sirach 30:14–15).

18

Make new friends

Some friends play at friendship, but a true friend sticks closer than one's nearest kin.
PROVERBS 18:24

One of the delights of ministry is to be at the centre of a large network of people where, give or take the odd individual, everybody wants to be the minister's friend. All that changes with retirement. Retirement for ministers means that we are no longer at the centre. Indeed, for most of us we are no longer there at all; we have moved away from our church, and as far as most ministers are concerned, we have moved away from the place where we were known. And in moving away we have lost some, if not many, of our friends.

One of the challenges of retirement is to make friends again. That is not easy, for the older we are, the more difficult making friends can be. Nonetheless, 'it is not good that… man should be alone' (Genesis 2:18). We need friends, real friends, the kind of friends about whom the book of Proverbs speaks: 'A friend loves at all times,' or in the words of the GNB, 'Friends always show their love' (Proverbs 17:17); 'Some friends play at friendship, but a true friend sticks closer than one's nearest kin,' or in the words of the GNB, 'Some friendships do not last, but some friends are more loyal than brothers' (Proverbs 18:24).

Friends make all the difference to living. I cannot imagine life without them. To quote Jesus son of Sirach again: 'Faithful friends are a sturdy shelter; whoever finds one has found a treasure. Faithful friends are beyond price; no amount can balance their worth. Faithful friends are life-saving medicine; and those who fear the Lord will find them' (Sirach 6:14–16).

There are, however, friends and friends. The word 'friend' can actually cover four different categories of friends:

1 Casual friends: acquaintances, people whose names we know.
2 General friends: people we might invite to our home for a party.
3 Good friends: people with whom we can begin to be open.
4 Close friends: our best friends, people with whom we can be completely 'real'.[118]

According to Oxford professor Richard Dunbar, the maximum number of friends for each category is 150 for casual friends, 50 for general friends, 15 for good friends and five for close friends.

Making new friends again is not easy for retired ministers. It is much more difficult making friends in later life than when we were young.[119] Nonetheless building friendships is what makes life worth living. In the words of Joan Chittister: 'At its core life is not about things, but about relationships… Relationships are the alchemy of life. They turn the dailiness into gold.'[120] However, building relationships takes time. Indeed, according to Professor Jeffrey Hall of the University of Kansas, it takes 90 hours for a person to become a good friend and another 110 hours for that person to become one of our closest buddies.[121]

Making friends in a new church is not always easy. When I moved to my current church, the first thing I did was to join two fellowship groups, with a view firstly to making new friends. Every Sunday I tried, and still try, to get to know one new name. I always have a card in my pocket to write a new name. The first Christmas after we joined the church we threw a party for 50 or so of these new friends, most of whom at that stage were really acquaintances. Gradually, many of those acquaintances have begun to become friends. Since then we have been invited into people's homes and to a range of social activities. I recognise, of course, that many retired ministers will not have the space or indeed the wherewithal to entertain 50 people, but that is not the point. What I am seeking to emphasise is that 'friendships don't just "happen". Friendship has to be sought, welcomed and built.'[122]

Making friends outside the church can be a challenge too. That is why when I was minister of my last church, I joined Rotary. I wanted not only to enjoy a weekly cooked English breakfast, but also to make friends beyond the church. Since retiring and having more time to spare, I became president of my Rotary club and got to know Rotarians in other clubs too. I joined a political party and extended my friendship circle even further. We belong to a wide range of networks, and as a result have many casual friends in the city in which we live.

Of course, not every retired minister will want to join Rotary, nor will they want to join a political party. However, there are plenty of other ways of interacting with people beyond the church. Joining a bowling club, becoming a member of a choir, belonging to a book club or attending study courses linked with the University of the Third Age are other possibilities. The challenge is to turn casual friends into good friends!

19

Reconnect with old friends

Do your best to come to me soon, for Demas, in love with this present world, has deserted me and gone to Thessalonica; Crescens has gone to Galatia, Titus to Dalmatia. Only Luke is with me. Get Mark and bring him with you, for he is useful in my ministry. I have sent Tychicus to Ephesus.

2 TIMOTHY 4:9–12

I think it is not an exaggeration to say that the apostle Paul not only valued friends, but he valued in particular friends of long standing. One of those long-standing friends was John Mark, with whom at one stage Paul fell out (Acts 13:13), but clearly the friendship had since been renewed and Paul was keen to have him with him, perhaps in order to take the place of Tychicus.

During the years of ministry, it is not always easy to hold on to old friends. Unlike most people, ministers still 'in harness' are not able to go away at weekends, for the focus is very much on the church. The only way in which we kept in touch with most of our friends was through an annual Christmas letter.

There is something special about old friends, for 'they have a memory of the same events and have the same mode of thinking'.[123] Unlike newer friends, there is no need for us to prove our worth with old friends; with them we can abandon pretence and be ourselves. Indeed, according to Ralph Waldo Emerson, 'It is one of the blessings of old friends that you can afford to be stupid with them.'[124] Old friends have stood the test of time. In this respect the words of Jesus son of Sirach come to mind: 'Do not abandon old friends, for new ones cannot equal them. A new friend is like new wine; when it has aged, you can drink it with pleasure' (Sirach 9:10).

Reconnecting with old friends is about laughing over old times and talking through the challenges we have faced over the years. In the first instance, it is a warm and positive experience as we remember what life was like so many years ago. It can also be humbling to discover how we have changed over the years; perhaps we no longer see life in the black-and-white terms of old. It can also be revealing, as we share confidences and reveal the lows as well as the highs of our lives.

Reconnecting with old friends is much easier than making new friends. It is amazing how quickly trust is restored and friendship is renewed. I'm told that it is even good for our mental health! Reconnecting is not to be feared, but to be looked forward to.

Retirement offers time and opportunity to reconnect with old friends, whether it is over a drink, a meal or even a weekend together. In the past few years, I have been taking the initiative and contacting old friends to see if they would be interested in meeting up again. Without exception, everybody has been very positive. Sometimes people have come to us; sometimes we have gone to them. Often it has involved me travelling up to London and sometimes further afield. Reconnecting involves effort and expense, but in every instance the effort and the expense have been worthwhile. Never have I found myself regretting the decision to reconnect. Much as I am grateful for new friends, there is something special, even precious, about old friends. It is only in meeting up with old friends, that I have discovered, as Stephen Sondheim put it, how much I missed them till now.[125]

20

Enjoy the grandchildren

Grandchildren are the crown of the aged.

PROVERBS 17:6

Just as in Old Testament times, so today not every older person has grandchildren. I recognise that there will inevitably be some readers who do not have children, let alone grandchildren. This is, therefore, very much an optional section, in which I seek to explore how retired ministers can make the most of the challenge – for a challenge it is – of relating to their grandchildren.

Grandchildren are special. As one wit put it, 'The idea that no one is perfect is a view most commonly held by people with no grandchildren.' On the other hand, there is truth in the observation that while 'an hour with your grandchildren can make you feel young again, anything longer than that, and you start to age quickly!'[126]

When Jemima, our first grandchild, was born, I read *Grandparenting: The agony and the ecstasy* by Jay Kessler.[127] I later wrote an article reflecting on five nuggets of wisdom I discovered there:

1 'We cannot stop the passage of time... We can merely learn to accept our new roles graciously.'[128] Yes, I said, there is wisdom in that. In one sense, few of us want to become grandparents: it's a sign that we are getting old. Yet none of us can turn the clock back. Far better to accept graciously the challenge of our new calling.

2 'We've had our shot at parenting. Now, as grandparents, we become a support to our children as they attempt the confusing and demanding task of parenting.'[129] That's so true. I guess I'll find that there are times when I am tempted to interfere in my grandchild's upbringing. But my new role is to affirm and cheer on her parents.

3 'We need to restore the values, loyalties and security of family life to provide an environment in which children can grow up safe and healthy to become what God intended them to be.'[130] Yes, indeed. Sadly, we live in a world where many families break down, where many grandchildren are confused and hurt and often filled with anger, resentment and perhaps even guilt as a result of their parents' divorce. In such situations grandparents have a special stabilising role to play.

4 'We can't change society. But what we can do, as grandparents, is to provide for them a solid moral framework, based on biblical principles, to help them establish their own moral standards.'[131] True again! We can't control what our grandchildren see and hear and experience. We can, however, listen. We can empathise with their struggles and offer them guidelines.

5 'We cannot spare them most of the struggles and failures of life. We can, however, demonstrate that after a long life filled with battles and victories, we can come out on the other side and do so with grace.'[132] Even more true! At the end of the day, grandchildren aren't impressed with grandparents who are forever moralising. What really counts is to see and hear how they have coped in the tough times, how their faith in God has enabled them to come through with a thankful and loving spirit.[133]

It is a real challenge to be a Christian grandparent. I read of an American Presbyterian minister working in a deprived area of New York who said: 'We never tell the kids to say "Our Father" in the Lord's Prayer, because most of their fathers are alcoholic or absent. The person who represents God to them most of all is their grandmother.' That is a sobering thought, but the truth is that grandmothers, and grandfathers for that matter, can have a real influence on their grandchildren's understanding of God. As Paul reminded his young friend Timothy, his faith had in the first place been shaped not just by his mother Eunice but also by his grandmother Lois (2 Timothy 1:5; see also 3:14).

How do we rise to the challenge before us? Let me share some very ordinary examples of how we try to bless our grandchildren by sharing our faith in a simple way:

- We pray for them. It has been said that the greatest gift we can give to our grandchildren is our time and our prayers.

- When they come to visit us, we always say grace at meals, and we try to begin the day with a prayer and a reading. We also pray with them before they go to sleep.

- In the spirit of the Shema (Deuteronomy 6:4–7), we make opportunities to talk to them about God and his love and about how God has shared his love with us through Jesus.

- If they are with us over a Sunday, we try to take them to church, but changing churches has made things difficult in that respect.

- With our encouragement, they all come to church on Christmas Day.

- We buy them Christian books and give them Christian Advent calendars and Fairtrade Christian Easter eggs, which tell the story of Easter.

- Before the grandchildren open their Christmas presents around the tree, we have developed a tradition that first I read Luke's account of the birth of Jesus (Luke 2:1–7), and then we pray together.

- We try to be creative in how we share our faith. One Easter, I emailed my grandchildren every day for 28 days. Each email contained a picture, a few verses of scripture and a prayer, featuring the Passion, death and resurrection of Jesus. Another year when for a period of seven weeks I was away in Australia and New Zealand, I sent them a weekly instalment of 'Grandpa's adventures'. Each instalment included a reflection on some aspect of God at work in his world. Another year, over a period of twelve weeks, I sent them a short Bible verse a week together with a comment, and suggested that they might learn the verses. Although not all the grandchildren learnt the verses, hopefully they were all helped to understand a little more of God's love for them.[134]

Precisely how we relate to our grandchildren will vary. So much depends on personality and circumstance. One thing, however, is clear: grandchildren can form a real 'mission field'. My research into retirement has shown that around half the grandchildren of retired ministers do not attend church.[135]

21

Tell your story

We will tell to the coming generation the glorious deeds of the Lord… and the wonders that he has done.
PSALM 78:4

For those with grandchildren, retirement is a wonderful opportunity to enjoy the grandchildren. What is more, along with all the fun and games, spending time with grandchildren gives us an opportunity to enter into the world of the young, and what an education our grandchildren can be! True, this is not always easy when grandchildren live at a distance, but the internet and social media can bridge the miles.

Along with the listening, we also have an opportunity to tell our story, by telling our grandchildren about our experience of life, and in so doing to leave a legacy of faith to the younger generation. In the first year of my retirement I drafted 'my story'. As I wrote in the introduction:

This account is written in the first place for my grandchildren. The day may come when they ask, 'Who was my grandfather? What kind of man was he? What did he do? What were the key influences upon his life?' As I look back on my own grandfathers, I wish I had probed into their backgrounds. I knew that my father's stepfather had fought at Gallipoli, yet it never occurred to me to ask Grandad what it had been like, let alone how that experience had scarred him for life. I knew that my mother's father had worked at St Pancras town hall in central London, but I never asked Grandpa what he did there. My grandfathers were simply my grandfathers, and that was it. Would that they had written a page or two about themselves! It is this experience of longing to know so much more about my grandfathers, which initially caused me to write *This Is My Story*.[136]

Later I revised the material and made the story more accessible to a wider public. However, *This Is My Story: A story of life, faith and ministry* was, and remains, primarily written for my grandchildren, in which I speak of what Jesus has meant and still means to me.

It is, of course, not just ministers with grandchildren who can tell their stories to the young. There may well be opportunities for ministers without grandchildren to do something similar, not least to the grandchildren of their friends.

Another way to tell your story for future generations is to write what Bruce and Katherine Epperly called a 'spiritual obituary':

While most published obituaries simply state the facts of a person's life in a dry fashion, a spiritual obituary enables the writer to look back upon her or his life and to look ahead toward the future in a way that enables the writer to see the interplay of the many values that shaped her or his life.[137]

They suggested that in a spiritual obituary we answer questions such as:

- What values have motivated your life?
- What is your image of God and how has it shaped your spiritual journey?
- What was your most heroic moment?
- What do you most want to celebrate in your life?
- What do you most want to celebrate in your ministry?
- Whom have you loved in the course of your life?
- What are your favourite hobbies and pastimes?

- What key phrases, scriptures or aphorisms sum up your life?
- What do you plan to do in the remaining years of your life?
- What value or counsel do you leave to the next generation?
- What causes have you devoted your life to?

If that all sounds too serious, then an alternative is to buy a 'journal of a lifetime' from a good stationery shop, and there sketch out some of the key events in your life.[138]

22

Share your faith

Come and hear… and I will tell what he has done for me.
PSALM 66:16

Sharing our faith is the business of a lifetime. Long before we were ordained, many of us shared our faith at our baptism or at our confirmation. Down through the years of our ministry we continued to share our faith. Now, as we are growing old, we still have a duty to share our faith with others. The psalmist encourages us to 'tell to the coming generation the glorious deeds of the Lord' (Psalm 78:4–6; see also Psalm 22:30–31; Psalm 48:13–14; Psalm 71:18), but we should also be mindful of our fellow 'seniors' who are perhaps more open to the gospel than any other age group. The older people become, the more frequently they experience life-changing events, such as the death of a spouse or of a close friend, a move into a retirement home or deterioration of health. These events provide windows of opportunity, in which people seem to move from resistance or indifference to the gospel to receptivity and openness.[139]

How do we share our faith at this stage of our lives? By telling our story! In the words of the chorus of the hymn 'Blessed Assurance', made popular by the Billy Graham crusades: 'This is my story, this is my song: praising my Saviour all the day long.' No, I don't have in mind a sung testimony, but rather a simple account of what Jesus means to us when people ask us about what we have done in life. In my experience, many people want to know what makes a minister tick. If we look for opportunities to share our faith, it is amazing how often they come.

Another great way for older people, and this includes retired ministers, to share their faith while also making friends is to join a book club. Book clubs are not just about literary criticism; they also inevitably involve regular discussions about values. I have friends in Australia who, upon moving to a retirement complex, set up a book club to which they could invite their new neighbours as the first thing they did.

Even if we become frail and are confined to a bedroom in a care home, we can speak of how we have experienced God's faithfulness to us down the years, and so share our faith with those who look after us and with family members too. Vernon Grounds commented:

> That is the message of Psalm 71. The older generation can pass on to the next generation... Perhaps a grandparent's congregation is one small grandchild, but how important it is that the upcoming generations hear about the spiritual experience of the older generations. The good news is that older people, if they look, can find opportunities for ongoing usefulness.[140]

23

Discover yourself

By the grace of God I am what I am.
1 CORINTHIANS 15:10

Telling your story can also be a way of discovering yourself, for as we look back we discover that telling our story gives meaning to our lives. In fact, according to Daniel Taylor, 'This desire for meaning is the originating impulse of story. We tell stories because we hope to find or create significant connections between things. Stories link past, present, and future in a way that tells us where we have been (even before we were born), where we are, and where we should be going'.[141] As the American psychiatrist Leslie Farber said:

> It is given to human experience not only to contemplate its own nature and existence but to historicize itself... As I survey this pastness that belongs to me alone, this unique tangle of public-private, shared-solitary, accidental-intentional, known-unknown, that is my life so far, and is in some way accountable for my arrival in this present, and for whatever present-ness is yet to come – what I long to find is some particularity, some singularity that makes it not only in fact, but in truth mine.[142]

I came across an article recently where the author stated that first and foremost we are not to view ourselves as *homo sapiens*, that is, a person able to think, but rather *homo narrans*, a person with a story to tell.[143] What's more, according to the Irish philosopher Richard Kearney, 'the untold story is not worth living'.[144] This in turn reminded me of Socrates, who, on trial before his fellow Athenians, declared, 'The unexamined life is not worth living.'

In my first church there was a young woman who, before she was even 30 years of age, had published her story. Although she had a fascinating story to tell of her conversion from Judaism to Christianity, it was just the beginning of her story. It is only when we are growing old that we can begin truly to tell our story and in so doing see ourselves as we are. In that regard the entertainer Joyce Grenfell in her old age said, 'The older you get, the more you realize that happiness is losing your false sense of what you are, your false self. What was that lovely quotation? Become what you are! Well, that interpreted means become what your true potential is, your spiritual wholeness.'[145] Sadly, not all older people are able to see themselves as they really are, let alone then find the courage to share their true self with others. But what a difference it makes when we can be real with ourselves and with others.

For the retired, said James Woodward, questions such as 'Who have I been? Who am I now? Who will I be? What will become of me?' are very significant.[146] He went on:

Older age, if nothing else, will provide a time to explore our undiscovered self. This might constitute a challenge, but ageing can be a pilgrimage and an opportunity to look inside at what we really believe to be true, what bothers us, and how we might make a difference in this particular stage of our lives.[147]

IV

Preparing for the final journey

24

Rise to the challenge of being

Abide in me as I abide in you.
JOHN 15:4

Jesus in the upper room spoke to his disciples of the importance of 'abiding' in him. Abiding should contain no strain or effort: it is rest from effort. The natural branch should not strain to remain a part of the vine: it simply is. All it needs to do is to stay connected. This priority never changes. Over the years I have preached many times on the need to be still and cultivate our relationship with Christ, and I have often quoted the words of Thomas Merton: 'Action is the stream and contemplation is the spring.'[148]

Yet, if truth be told, learning to 'be' is a challenge for an activist like me. Indeed, it seems to be a challenge for most retired ministers, not least because we have often defined ourselves by what we do. On retiring, for instance, I could no longer use as my email signature 'Senior minister of Central Baptist Church, Chelmsford'; instead I used 'Chairman of *Ministry Today UK* and chairman of the College of Baptist Ministers'. Then, on becoming president of my Rotary club, I added 'president of the Rotary Club of Chelmsford Rivermead'. Fortunately, I realised the nonsense of my ways: I was defining myself by what I did, rather than by who I was. At that point I did away with all such pretence.

Retirement is the last opportunity to rise to the challenge of being. Indeed, sometimes the limitations of older age force us to rise to this challenge. At my last appraisal the external ministerial facilitator began by asking, 'Paul, what are your plans for retirement?' After I had outlined my plans, he asked a second question: 'Paul, how will you cope if you have a major stroke within the first year of your retirement?' In a memorable way, he underlined the fact that ultimately God calls us to 'be' and not to 'do'.

Although growing older is not synonymous with ill health, sooner or later our health will become an issue; to pretend otherwise is a form of self-delusion. One day, unless God takes us early, we shall make the transition from the 'third age' of active retirement to the 'fourth age' of dependency. Then many of us will begin to experience the trials of old age as depicted by the Teacher in Ecclesiastes:

> Remember your Creator while you are still young, before those dismal days and years come when you will say, 'I don't enjoy life.' That is when the light of the sun, the moon, and the stars will grow dim for you, and the rain clouds will never pass away. Then your arms, that have protected you, will tremble, and your legs, now strong, will grow weak. Your teeth will be too few to chew your food, and your eyes too dim to see clearly. Your ears will be deaf to the noise of the street. You will barely be able to hear the mill as it grinds or music as it plays, but even the song of a bird will wake you from sleep. You will be afraid of high places, and walking will be dangerous. Your hair will turn white; you will hardly be able to drag yourself along, and all desire will be gone.
>
> We are going to our final resting place, and then there will be mourning in the streets. The silver chain will snap, and the golden lamp will fall and break; the rope at the well will break, and the water jar will be shattered. Our bodies will return to the dust of the earth, and the breath of life will go back to God, who gave it to us.
>
> ECCLESIASTES 12:1–7 (GNB)

The point to grasp here is that the Teacher is not revelling in death; rather he is encouraging his readers to make the most of life. The emphasis is not so much *memento mori* (remember we will all die) but *carpe diem* (seize the day). How do we seize the day? How do we rise to this challenge of old age? In the words of Paul Tournier, 'What is important for the aged is not what they are still able to do, nor yet what they have accumulated and cannot take with them. It is what they are.'[149] Or as he wrote on another occasion:

> From then on a man's value is judged not by what he does, but by what he is, not by the position he occupies or by his titles, but by his personal maturity, by his breadth of mind, by his inner life, by the quality of his love for others, and by the intrinsic, and not the market, value of what he brings into the world.[150]

Tournier was right: so many older people, including some of us retired ministers, fail to reach that point of understanding and maturity.

Paul Clayton, an American minister in the United Church of Christ, helpfully developed that point in his book on ministers finding meaning in retirement. In a chapter entitled 'Don't just do something, stand there', he said:

> We are called not only to do God's work in the world, but also to be God's people in the world... That identity is marked by integrity rather than greed, care for others rather than self-absorption, humility rather than arrogance.[151]

When illness strikes and death looms and there is nothing we can do, what counts is our 'witness of courage and faith'.[152]

I find myself greatly challenged by what Clayton had to say. If my experience of church life is anything to go by, far too much ministry to seniors involves entertaining the elderly rather than helping them to face the challenges presented by their mortality. Similarly, my experience of meetings for retired ministers is that we do not talk about how we cope spiritually as we become more limited physically. Our comfort at this time should be that 'even though our outer nature is wasting away, our inner nature is being renewed day by day' (2 Corinthians 4:16).[153]

25

Learn contentment

I have learned to be content with whatever I have… I can do all things through him who strengthens me.
PHILIPPIANS 4:11, 13

David Winter wrote of 'serenity' as being 'the most attractive feature of the elderly'.[154] Unfortunately, serenity is sometimes lacking in those of us in older years. Gordon Rupp in one of his sermons quoted the results of an American study into people aged 85 and over, which distinguished three groups of people: the Angry Ones, the Rocking Chair People and the Mature:

> The Angry Ones were pathetic and disturbing, because we have all met people who seem to have become sour and embittered, disillusioned and resentful as they grow old. They have accumulated frustrations, they are nostalgic or guilty, they become a trial to those about them, and their tempers range from general grumpiness to downright nastiness.[155]

When we are tempted to grumble, perhaps we should pray the Nun's Prayer:

> Lord, Thou knowest better than I know myself that I am growing older and will some day be old. Keep me from the fatal habit of thinking I must say something on every subject and on every occasion. Release me from craving to straighten out everybody's affairs. Make me thoughtful but not moody; helpful but not bossy. With my vast store of wisdom it seems a

pity not to use it at all, but Thou knowest Lord that I want a few friends at the end.

Keep my mind free from the recital of endless details; give me wings to get to the point. Seal my lips on my aches and pains. They are increasing and love of rehearsing them is becoming sweeter as the years go by. I dare not ask for grace enough to enjoy the tales of others' pains, but help me to endure them with patience.

I dare not ask for improved memory but for a growing humility and a lessening cocksureness when my memory seems to clash with the memories of others. Teach me the glorious lesson that occasionally I may be mistaken.

Keep me reasonably sweet; I do not want to be a saint – some of them are hard to live with – but a sour old person is one of the crowning works of the devil. Give me the ability to see good things in unexpected places and talents in unexpected people. And, give me, O Lord, the grace to tell them so. Amen.[156]

We need to learn to be content and to come to that point where we can say with the apostle Paul: 'I have learned to be content with whatever I have… I can do all things through him who strengthens me' or, in the words of the GNB, 'I have learned to be satisfied with what I have… I have the strength to face all conditions by the power that Christ gives me' (Philippians 4:11, 13). It is important to note that Paul's contentment or sufficiency was rooted in Jesus. By contrast, the underlying Greek word here (*autarkeia*), variously translated as 'contentment' or 'sufficiency', was used by the Stoics to describe people who through self-discipline had become independent of their external circumstances, who had discovered within themselves resources that were more than adequate for any situation that might arise. Epictetus, for instance, described the road to Stoic contentment or self-sufficiency in this way:

Begin with a cup or a household utensil; if it breaks, say 'I don't care'. Go on to a horse or pet dog; if anything happens to it, say 'I don't care'. Go on to yourself, and if you are hurt or injured in any way, say 'I don't care'. If you go on for long enough, you will come to a stage when you can watch your nearest and dearest suffer and die, and say 'I don't care'.[157]

Unlike the Stoics, whose 'contentment' lay in screwing up themselves in an act of deliberate self-will, Paul's 'contentment' was not to be found in himself, but in Jesus. Paul was not self-sufficient; he was Christ-sufficient. This contentment, however, does not come automatically: it needs to be learnt. Walter Hansen commented:

> The emphatic use of the personal pronoun *I* highlights his claim that he did his homework, mastered his lessons, and passed his tests. Although the attitude of contentment was not natural nor did it come easily, this quality of contentment eventually became an essential attribute of his character.[158]

United with Christ, the source of absolute power, Paul was able to face life and whatever it might throw at him. It was Paul's experience that it was precisely in his time of greatest need, in his moment of utter weakness, that he experienced the power of Christ to the full. For it was when he was troubled by his thorn in the flesh that the Lord said to him, 'My grace is sufficient for you, for power is made perfect in weakness.' To which Paul added: 'For whenever I am weak, then I am strong' (2 Corinthians 12:9–10).

This contentment in old age was exemplified in the life of the former journalist and broadcaster Malcolm Muggeridge, who was a difficult, irascible man until he found faith in Christ towards the end of his life. When he first became aware of the onset of old age, he wrote:

> As the old do, I often wake up in the night and feel myself, in some curious way, half in and half out of my body, so that I seem to be hovering between the sheets and seeing in the darkness and the distance a glow in the sky, the lights of Augustine's City of God. In that condition, when it seems a toss-up whether I return to my body to live out another

day, or make off, there are two particular conclusions, two extraordinarily sharp impressions that come to me. The first is that of the incredible beauty of our earth – its colours and shapes, its smells and its features, of the enchantment of human love and companionship, and of the blessed fulfilment provided by human work and human procreation. And the second, a certainty surpassing all words and thoughts, that as an infinitesimal particle of God's creation, I am a participant in his purposes, which are loving and not malign, creative and not destructive, orderly and not chaotic, universal and not particular. And in that certainty, a great peace and joy.[159]

Gaining such contentment is not always easy, especially when life becomes increasingly restricted and a debilitating illness perhaps strikes. I think of a retired minister whose wife has just been diagnosed with Parkinson's and of all the adjustments they now have to make. At such a time one can perhaps only pray the 'serenity prayer' of Reinhold Niebuhr:

God, grant me the serenity
To accept the things I cannot change,
Courage to change the things I can,
And wisdom to know the difference.[160]

26

Acknowledge your mortality

So teach us to count our days that we may gain a wise heart.
PSALM 90:12

Even before ill health sets in, let alone a diagnosis of a potentially fatal disease occurs, we need to take on board our mortality. As Christians we are called to live life in the light of eternity. For myself, ever since the beginning of retirement I have identified with the words of Simeon, who, on encountering the infant Jesus in the temple, said in the traditional words of the *Book of Common Prayer*: 'Lord, now lettest thou thy servant depart in peace.' Actually, what appears to be a prayer is a statement: literally, 'you are letting your servant depart in peace'. The present tense may emphasise that Simeon senses his impending death and is ready for it. In today's terms we might say that his bucket list was complete.

We could add that he was at peace not just with God, but also with himself. He had come to the point where he no longer needed to strive: he was now able to die well. He was ready to 'depart' – just as the apostle Paul was also ready to (see 2 Timothy 4:6, where Paul employs a similar metaphor). It is in that sense that I identify with Simeon. I have lived a full life and see no reason for a bucket list, even though I am still happy to travel to new destinations. In God's good time I feel I am ready to go, because I have received the assurance of God's promises in Jesus.

On the other hand, I like the suggestion that Simeon here provides not so much a model for dying as for living. Was Simeon simply affirming that when the time came for him to die, God was allowing him to depart in peace because he had seen in Christ the fulfilment of his hopes? 'So,' concluded Martin Parsons, 'when we sing the *Nunc dimittis* we are not asking to die, but proclaiming our readiness for the call when it comes.'[161] We, like Simeon, have 'received' the Lord Jesus (the same Greek word used in Luke 2:28 is found in John 1:12), and that makes all the difference in the world. My mind goes to Cicely Saunders, the founder of the modern hospice movement, who said, 'We will do all we can not only to help you die peacefully, but also to live until you die.'[162]

But one day we shall die. As the psalmist reminds us, the God who breathed life into the dust (Genesis 2:7) will 'turn us back to dust' (Psalm 90:3). Our lives 'are like a dream, like grass… in the morning it flourishes and is renewed; in the evening it fades and withers' (Psalm 90:5–6). Thank God, that is not the end of the story, for although 'all die in Adam, so all will be made alive in Christ' (1 Corinthians 15:22). Death is not the end, and yet we need to face up to the fact that in the light of eternity our lives are but fleeting. In spite of that which we have achieved in God's service, we shall soon be forgotten.

This was underlined for me when I revisited the town where for over 13 years I had been the minister of the local Baptist church. I knew the front of the church premises had undergone some alterations, so I decided to call and see for myself the changes that had been made. It was a weekday, so I had to knock on the side door to get in. A pleasant lady answered the door, but she hadn't a clue who I was – nor indeed did any of the other staff in the church office. I was amazed. Under my leadership a small declining church had developed into a strong, vibrant one. In those 13 years the church had quadrupled in size, from 83 to over 300 members. God had really blessed my ministry, and many people had been won to Christ and been baptised. But now, some 30 years later, not even my name was known!

My initial reaction was to feel a little depressed. I thought back on all the time and the effort, the pain and the tears, the struggle and the sacrifice of my 43 years of service as an ordained Christian minister. Was it all for nothing? No, of course not! Although my life and my work may indeed be soon forgotten, I dare to believe that my ministry has had eternal consequences. Precisely what those consequences are, I do not know. In this life it is impossible for any minister to measure what God has achieved through them. For the most part we have little, if any, knowledge of what has been wrought in other people's lives. Yet the reality is that time and again in my ministry and indeed the ministry of every other minister too, 'the kingdom of God has come near' (see Luke 10:9). Although the time comes when our names are forgotten and our achievements are no longer known, in the sight of eternity we have made a mark that will last. Our lives will not have been lived in vain. God willing, the day will come when the Lord, whose 'steadfast love… is from everlasting to everlasting' (Psalm 103:17), will say to me, and to many, many others, 'Well done, good and faithful servant… Come and share your master's happiness' (Matthew 25:21, 23, NIV).

27

Keep on believing

Do not let your hearts be troubled. Believe in God, believe also in me. In my Father's house there are many dwelling-places.
JOHN 14:1-2

As I reviewed the previous chapter, I became conscious that some readers will have lost their life partner and will be all too painfully aware of the fragility of life. It is one thing to lose a father or mother, but to be 'robbed' of a husband or a wife is a far more devastating and agonising experience. In such a context, I find the words of Jesus spoken to his disciples the night before he died a great help: 'Do not let your hearts be troubled. Believe in God' (John 14:1). Or rather, 'Stop letting your hearts be in a turmoil – instead, keep on believing in God.' For in the underlying Greek we have two present imperatives, implying an ongoing action. The pain of grief is ongoing, and so faith needs to be ongoing too.

Death is a nasty business. It is an 'enemy' (1 Corinthians 15:26). In the words of the great Swiss psychiatrist Carl Jung:

> Death is indeed a piece of brutality. There is no sense in pretending otherwise. It is brutal not only as a physical event but far more so psychically: a human being is torn away from us, and what remains is the icy stillness of death.[163]

To lose a husband or a wife when they could have had many more years of life ahead of them feels damnably unfair of God. For most of us, faith, initially, does not make the pain any better.

Contrary to what some people imagine, being a minister does not make it any easier. As I write I have before me a letter from a retired minister, which tells of his ongoing struggle to cope with the loss of his wife of 40 years and of how his faith has been tested. At the time he felt that God was stripping his emotions 'like the layers of an onion'. He wrote: 'All of the defences that I had so carefully built up over the years to protect myself from further pain in ministry God was laying bare until my very core was reached', and only 'then could the reconstruction of my life begin'.

One of the most moving books I have read is *23 Days: A story of love, death and God* by Francis Bridger, an Anglican minister, who told the story of how his wife Renée was diagnosed with terminal cancer and then 23 days later was dead. Francis Bridger recounted the devastating grief he experienced.

> Grief has only one goal: to usurp your love's place. It wants to become your new companion, your new best friend. This is what it lusts after. But – and here's the real cruelty – it doesn't even attempt to play the seductress, enticing you into its presence with promises of consolation. No, it waits in hiding until it can steal up, knock you to the ground and stamp all over you as you writhe in agony. Then it delights in kicking the living hell out of you until your guts are bursting and you can take no more, leaving you a sobbing wreck crying out in desperation for your loved one to hold you in her arms and make everything right. But, of course, she can't. How I hate that bloody cancer.[164]

Bridger experienced death in the raw. But it is not just a story of love and death; it is also a story of God. Bridger railed against God – and understandably so. Yet, in the midst of his despair, he discovered that God had not abandoned him:

> In the midst of human emotions of the most overwhelming kind, it is possible to know God... He enfolds our emotions, however negative, in his love and deals gently with them. He

does not leave us or forsake us, whatever our feelings might tell us. And he does not desert us because we express them honestly. As I have discovered, it is in the storm centre of confusion and pain that he meets us... He invites us to discover him there... It is an awesome and challenging thought.[165]

There are no easy answers as to why God 'allows' our loved one to die. But as Christians, we do know that God loves us and that there is nothing which can ever separate us from his love (see Romans 8:38–39). At such a time we need to 'keep on believing', and as we do so, we will find, as Bridger and many others too have found, that God is there for us.

28

Put things in order

Thus says the Lord: Set your house in order, for you shall die; you shall not recover.
ISAIAH 38:1

I made my first will at the age of 25, just before we set out to serve God with the Baptist Missionary Society in Congo/Zaire, and in more recent years I have given to my children power of attorney relating to both finance and health. Both the making of a will and the giving the power of attorney to loved ones seem to me to be essential steps in setting our affairs in order.

Understandably, with ministers often having to deal with the dying and the bereaved, almost 90% of those who responded to my survey on how ministers experience retirement had made a will.[166] By contrast, in 2016 36% of over-55s in the UK had not made a will. However, I was a little surprised that three-quarters of retired ministers in my survey had not given power of attorney (for health and welfare and/or for property and financial affairs), for it ensures that one's wishes are observed when one is no longer able to care for oneself.[167]

As part of putting things in order, I have filled in for my children an A4 booklet, 'My documents: what I own and where it is kept'. It lists such details as national insurance and passport numbers, names and contact details of our doctors, our accountant, our financial advisor and our solicitor; the date of our will, where it has been lodged and who the executors are; the dates of our powers of attorney and who the attorneys are; people and institutions to be contacted on our death; details relating to bank and building society accounts and also to pensions we receive; and a host of miscellaneous data such as energy providers and insurers for house and car. Copies of 'My documents' are already in the hands of our executors. In addition, I have drawn up a separate list of my passwords and other such information needed for this electronic age, and this list has also been given to those who in due course will need to use this information. Needless to say, the booklet and the list of passwords need to be regularly updated.

Another aspect of putting our affairs in order is planning our funeral. What a difference it can make for those who are left to know our favourite hymns and readings. For instance, my mother, who is almost blind, has chosen for her funeral a song by the blind hymn writer Frances van Alstyne (1820–1915), which looks forward to the day when, in the words of the chorus, we 'shall see him face to face'. Or as the last two lines of the final verse declare, on that day 'when my Saviour I will greet, my faith will then be changed to sight'. Interestingly, just over a third of retired ministers in my survey had chosen hymns or readings for their funeral. One respondent commented: 'Every time I try, new songs emerge that I prefer!'[168]

Some ministers might wish to plan their own funeral service. In this regard it is helpful to bear in mind that a funeral service should:

- initiate the healing energies of bereavement
- soothe the wounds of grief
- speak directly to the mourners
- offer something that unites rather than separates
- offer reflections that are a tapestry of the person's life, including both good and bad points
- encourage the message of hope
- state clearly that the person is dead to this life
- recognise the new role of the surviving partner (if applicable)
- unfreeze the numbness of grief[169]

Some years ago I drew up an order of service in which I set out the three hymns I want to be sung at my funeral: 'For all the love which from our earliest days';[170] 'Who would true valour see';[171] and 'I love you, O Lord, you alone'.[172] Along with Psalm 23 (God cares for us), John 14:1–2, 6 (Jesus calls us to trust him) and 1 Corinthians 15:20, 42–43, 54–57 (Paul works out the implications of the resurrection for us), I also chose 2 Corinthians 4:1–15 (treasure in clay jars) and requested that the preacher on that occasion takes this final passage as his text that day. In addition, I chose two special pieces of music: first, as an organ prelude, 'How beautiful are the feet of those who proclaim good news' from Handel's *Messiah* and then as an organ postlude, the Toccata from Widor's *Symphony for Organ No. 5*, which was played at our wedding.

But there is more to the funeral than an order of service. Bill Kirkpatrick told the story of a man who had been in the catering industry and who wished his friends to toast him with a glass of champagne. So, after the words of committal, the mourners were invited to surround the bier. Chilled champagne and glasses were wheeled in on a serving trolley, corks popped, glasses filled and passed around, and everyone drank a toast to the man's life as the coffin was lowered![173] Although such a suggestion may sound a little extreme, the concept of planning how others will remember us on the day of our funeral is important.

In my own case I have specified the name of the undertaker I wish to be used. I have asked that the newspaper death announcement includes a quotation from 1 Corinthians 15:57. I have given instructions for a committal service at the crematorium to precede the service of thanksgiving:

> Cheapest coffin. One floral tribute (not to be left at crematorium). If desired, money in lieu of flowers to be given to an organisation such as the Baptist Missionary Society. Organ music or recording of Brahms' *German Requiem* ('Death, where is your victory?'). The brief service to begin with one hymn:

'I will sing the wondrous story'. Include in the service Romans 14:7, a text given to me when I was baptised at Salemskapelle, Zurich.

In addition, I have asked that after the service there is a tea party to which all who attend the funeral service are to be invited: 'Let it be characterised by something outrageous, which indicates that in the midst of life's pain, there can be fun too: e.g. balloons!'

As for the disposal of ashes I have stated: 'No special service is required – probably Caroline would prefer to have them buried in a lawn cemetery, which she might wish to visit occasionally.' Needless to say, in making these plans there should always be an element of flexibility. Our loved ones need to know that they have the freedom to ignore some of our wishes!

As James White helpfully commented: 'Making plans for one's funeral is not necessarily a morbid preoccupation; it can be a witness to one's faith and a splendid way to advance in understanding of life.'[174] Indeed, for ministers, says Paul Clayton, 'to speak of death is not a depressing endeavour; it is to explore still another expression of our calling'.[175] All the more reason, perhaps, for this topic of 'putting things in order' to be on the agenda of meetings for retired ministers. In this way we can encourage one another and help one another (and our loved ones) to prepare for the day when God will take us to himself. In this way we will then be able to say with Pope John XXIII, 'My bags are packed. I am ready to leave.'[176]

29

Thank God for his goodness

**Bless the Lord, O my soul, and do not forget all his benefits –
who forgives all your iniquity, who heals all your diseases,
who redeems your life from the Pit, who crowns you with
steadfast love and mercy, who satisfies you with good as long
as you live, so that your youth is renewed like the eagle's.**
PSALM 103:2–5

'A true Christian,' wrote John Baillie, a Scottish theologian, 'is a man
[sic] who never for a moment forgets what God has done for him in
Christ and whose whole comportment and whose activity have their
root in the sentiment of gratitude.'[177] What is true of the Christian life
in general seems to me to be particularly apposite for Christians as
they begin to prepare for their final journey. The very act of recalling
God's goodness to us in former days reminds us that the God who
blessed us in the past will also be there to bless us in the present
and in the future. Thanking God for his goodness enables us to face
up to any worries and anxieties we may have as we contemplate
leaving our loved ones and begin what may appear to be a lonely
walk through the valley of the shadow of death.

In this regard I find it significant that Bruce and Katherine Epperly
encouraged retired ministers to become thankful people:

> Thanksgiving is the cornerstone of a well-lived life. We can
> move ahead to an unknown future with confidence precisely
> because we have experienced moments of grace and gratitude
> in the course of our lives. As you look back over your life's

journey, for what relationships and events are you most thankful? In your current life, what are the grace notes and joys for which you are thankful? For what persons in your life do you feel most grateful? For what opportunities are you most thankful? For what 'failures' are you most thankful?[178]

Here are helpful questions we all need to address. In the first instance, we can make a list of the many ways in which God has blessed us in our ministries, as also in life in general. We can make a list, too, of people who have been a blessing to us, and then perhaps write a personal note to each individual, thanking them for all that they meant to us (if some are no longer alive, then we could write to a member of their family). This writing of letters could be linked to Lent and could involve writing a letter a day to 40 people who have made a positive difference to our lives. It would be quite a challenge!

I concluded my autobiography by listing a series of things for which I am grateful to God. For instance, I thank God for:

- his amazing love for me seen above all in Jesus. What a difference Jesus makes to living (and, of course, to dying too).
- the family in which I grew up, and the love and security which they gave me.
- Caroline and the family which is now ours, and the love and support that I have received from them.
- the many friends who have enriched our lives, as also those friends who are still there for us.
- the privilege of having been a pastor. It is undoubtedly the most wonderful calling in the world.

In thanking God, we are making ourselves conscious that God is with us. He is in control, and however much we may have failed him, he will never fail us. Praising God for all his benefits to us is a help to dying well.

30

Let go of past hurts

Father, forgive them; for they do not know what they are doing.
LUKE 23:34

Another spiritual practice for what the Epperlys described as 'the winter in ministry' is the practice of forgiveness:

> In the course of a ministerial adventure, at one time or another, most pastors have felt misunderstood, attacked, neglected, treated unjustly, or professionally abused. You bear the scars of unhealed wounds that shape your current experiences of ministry. These same wounds will shape your attitude to church during your retirement.[179]

Ministry can be tough. Some years ago I undertook a survey of 141 ministers and 112 lay leaders within mainline Protestant denominations, and then wrote up the results in *Power for God's Sake: The use and abuse of power in the local church*. Key findings included: 'Churches treat us badly,' say nine out of ten ministers; most ministers under the age of 45 have considered giving up their calling; one in six ministers leave their churches in 'unhappy circumstances'. On the last point, I believe the number was actually higher, for 53% of Baptist ministers (and 43% of ministers in general) said that their predecessor had left the church in 'unhappy circumstances'.

These findings were confirmed in my interviews with retired Baptist ministers. Almost all of them had known tough times in ministry.

Some had known the pain of rejection and dismissal. It is no exaggeration to say that there are a large number of hurt ministers around. Yet if they are to live well in retirement and finally die well, they need to let go of the hurt and forgive, however unfairly or unjustly they may feel they were treated. What's more, they need to take the initiative in forgiving. There is little likelihood now that anyone will come and say sorry.

Forgiveness is a mark of a disciple of Jesus Christ. Jesus taught us to pray: 'Forgive us our sins, as we forgive others' (see Luke 11:4; Matthew 6:12). Jesus also said, 'Whenever you stand praying, forgive, if you have anything against anyone; so that your Father in heaven may also forgive you your trespasses' (Mark 11:25), and that the forgiveness of others is to be unlimited (Matthew 18:22; see also Luke 17:3–4).

There are eight principles underlying the call of Jesus to forgive:

1 **To forgive is to be forgiven.** The lesson of the parable of the unforgiving debtor (Matthew 18:23–35) is that an unforgiving spirit on our part indicates that we have never truly repented of our own sin. As John Stott put it, 'Once our eyes have been opened to see the enormity of our offence against God, the injuries which others have done to us appear by comparison extremely trifling. If, on the other hand, we have an exaggerated view of the offences of others, it proves that we have minimized our own.'[180] To speak in picture terms, we cannot receive forgiveness if our fists are clenched and our arms folded tightly round ourselves – for 'God gives where he finds empty hands' (Augustine).

2 **To forgive is not to excuse.** This is the lesson of the cross. When God forgave us, he did not excuse us. Instead God took our sin so seriously that he sent his Son to die in our place, to bear in his own body the punishment due to each one of us. So C.S. Lewis wrote: 'Forgiving does not mean excusing. Many people seem to think it does. They seem to think that if you ask them to forgive someone

who has cheated or bullied them, you are trying to make out that there was really no cheating or no bullying. But if that were so, there would be nothing to forgive. To be a Christian means to forgive the inexcusable, because God has forgiven the inexcusable in you.'[181]

3   **To forgive is to let go.** The Greek word translated 'to forgive' (*aphiemi*) literally means 'to let go, to allow to depart, to dismiss'. Not to forgive is to hold on to the injustice and the hurt. To forgive is to allow the anger and the pain to surface, for we need to face up to the truth of the damage done to us, and then to let go.

4   **To forgive does not always mean to forget.** There are times when it is neither realistic nor right to believe that we can forget the wrong done to us. The emotional wounds suffered from an act of wrongdoing may be so deep that it can take years before they heal. A scab and then a scar may form over the wound, but there may well always be a tenderness remaining, with the result that the wound can be reopened with ease. Furthermore, the effects of a wrongdoing may remain with us. There are times when, as a result of a wrong done, life is never the same. And, of course, it may just be right not to forget. Helmut Thielicke, a German pastor-theologian who endured the darkest days of the Nazi Third Reich, said, 'One should never mention the words "forgive" and "forget" in the same breath.'[182]

5   **To forgive often means that we take the initiative.** If God had waited for us to say sorry, then there would have been no cross. We see this too in the cry of Jesus from the cross: 'Father, forgive them; for they do not know what they are doing' (Luke 23:34).[183] Here we have what William Willimon called 'pre-emptive forgiveness', for Jesus prays for forgiveness before the perpetrators of this crime acknowledge their wrongdoing.[184] A failure on the part of the offending party to see their need of forgiveness does not lessen our need to forgive. Sometimes it is precisely the fact that we are willing to forgive which shames the other to say sorry.

6 **To forgive often involves a process.** We see this perhaps in the use of the present tense in the Lukan version of the Lord's Prayer (Luke 11:4), which may be translated as a continuous tense: 'as we keep forgiving'. We see this too in the prayer of Jesus from the cross (Luke 23:34); strictly speaking the Greek imperfect tense (*elegon*) that Luke uses should be translated 'Jesus was saying', rather than the simple past tense adopted by our English versions ('Jesus said'). The tense suggests an ongoing action in the past, rather than a one-off action. Jesus may have repeatedly prayed for forgiveness of those responsible for crucifying him as each of the nails was being driven in. There may well be a lesson here for us if we are to forgive others. Where pain and hurt are ongoing, sometimes we need to forgive and forgive and forgive. Forgiveness is often an ongoing process.

7 **To forgive is in the first instance an act of the will: 'I will forgive, in spite of the hurt and pain I feel.'** This is well illustrated by Corrie ten Boom when she was faced by one of her former SS guards from the Ravensbrück concentration camp, where she and her sister, Betsie, had been sent for harbouring Jews and where Betsie had died. She had just finished preaching at a church service when the ex-guard came forward. After beaming and bowing, he said: 'How grateful I am for your message, Fräulein. To think that, as you say, he has washed my sins away!' He told her that he had become a Christian, and he thrust his hand forward to shake hers, seeking her forgiveness as God had forgiven him. Her heart sank and she kept her hand by her side. She could not respond, as the memories of Ravensbrück came flooding back. While anger and vengeful thoughts boiled through her, she saw the sinfulness of them. She prayed for God's forgiveness towards her and for his help in forgiving the guard. She could not feel anything, not even the slightest spark of warmth. Again she prayed a silent prayer asking Jesus to give her his forgiveness. As she felt able to take his hand, she felt in her heart a love and a warmth which seemed to flood her whole being, bringing tears to her eyes.[185] Forgiveness here clearly involved an act of the will.

8 **To forgive is to be liberated from the destructive forces of our anger and pain.** Richard Nixon was right when he said, 'Always remember, others may hate you, but those who hate you don't win unless you hate them – and then you destroy yourself.'[186] Not to forgive, not to let go, is to allow the past to control us. To forgive is to bring about healing in our own lives, for when we forgive, the poison of bitterness and hate leaves the system. To forgive can also bring about healing in the lives of others. Margaret Magdalen, commenting on the prayer of Jesus, wrote: 'Forgiveness releases a power that can only be described as spiritually therapeutic… Think… of the marriages healed through forgiveness, the churches united through mutual forgiveness, the friendships remade through forgiveness.'[187] We are never the losers when we forgive; rather, we are always the winners.[188]

As Jesus prayed 'Father, forgive', so too ministers need to pray 'Father, forgive'.

31

Letting go and holding on

I press on to take hold of that for which Christ Jesus took hold of me.

PHILIPPIANS 3:12 (NIV)

As the apostle Paul looked ahead to the prize of eternal life, he knew the importance of holding on to the one who had taken hold of him. The time eventually comes for us to leave this world. In this regard I find it significant that when Paul spoke of his departure (Philippians 1:23; 2 Timothy 4:6) he used a word (*analusis/analusai*) which literally means a separation of one item from another and which can denote the loosening of a ship from its moorings. This word for 'casting off' was often used as a euphemism for death. In the ancient classical world, dying was viewed as a voyage down the river Styx into the underworld. Coins were placed in the eyes of the deceased to pay the ferry pilot, who would give the dead person passage into the afterlife. However, over against the pagans of his day, Paul had a much more positive view of death. He looked forward to making the journey across the sea of death into the haven of eternity, where on his arrival he would be 'with Christ' (Philippians 1:23).[189]

Charles Henry Brent (1862–1929), a bishop in the American Episcopal Church, went to the heart of the metaphor when he wrote:

What is dying? I am, standing on the seashore. A ship sails to the morning breeze and starts for the ocean. She is an object of beauty and I stand watching her till at last she fades on the horizon and someone at my side says, 'She is gone.' Gone where? Gone from my sight, that is all... Just at the moment when someone at my side says, 'she is gone,' there are others who are watching her coming, and other voices take up a glad shout, 'There she comes,' and that is dying.[190]

The reality, however, is that not all Christians look forward to dying. According to a survey of attitudes to death in the UK in 2018, some 34% of Christians felt unable even to talk about death with their family or with friends.[191] It may well be that some, even though they know that 'the sting' of death can be removed through faith in the crucified and risen Lord Jesus (1 Corinthians 15:56–57), have yet to learn to truly put their trust in Jesus. For them death is still 'the king of terrors' (Job 18:14; see also Psalm 55:4). They have perhaps yet to discover that Jesus, by destroying the one who has the power of death, has freed those 'who all their lives were held in slavery by the fear of death' (Hebrews 2:15).

Yet for others it may well be that they fear not so much death itself as the process of dying. This fear of dying is often linked with a fear of pain, loss of control of bodily functions, dementia and mental deterioration, and the embarrassment of potential total dependence. Thankfully, through the support of doctors and nurses, strategies can be developed to help the dying to cope with death, but even so we are still called to exercise faith and courage.[192]

Even then, some committed Christians find the thought of 'casting off' not easy to accept. David Frampton, a former palliative care specialist at St Joseph's Hospice, Farleigh Hospice and Mid-Essex Hospitals, wrote of how some Christians find it difficult to let go:

They continue to talk about getting better in spite of objective evidence of deterioration... Sadly, often such people 'die badly'. They are like someone standing on a jetty with one foot in a boat and one on land. As the two drift apart, there comes a point where the tension will no longer hold, and in dying patients, this may be resolved by a retreat from reality into confusion and unreachable anxiety. Here the only useful answer could be appropriate sedation.

Frampton went on to instance three 'experienced charismatic Christian leaders' finding themselves in such a situation, for each believed that they would be miraculously healed:

> With one of them, who had been a blessing to many people, it ended badly. The other two, toward the end, came to the reluctant and dislocating conclusion that, somehow, they had got it wrong, but were able, peacefully, to let go into the hands of the God they didn't now understand.[193]

Christians today, including ministers, need to rediscover what Christians of earlier times called the 'art of dying' (*ars moriendi*). In the Middle Ages and well into the 17th and 18th centuries many guides were produced to help people to die well. Today that 'art' has been largely lost, and dying has become a medical rather than a spiritual experience. As John Wyatt, a distinguished medical professor, said, instead of being 'passive and helpless recipients' of medical care, we need to become 'active participants in the process of dying'.[194] Of course, there is a place for medical help, but being sedated up to the eyeballs is not the ideal way to die. Instead, we should be allowed to slip away, conscious in the first place of God's presence, and conscious too of the presence of loved ones.

Dying well involves accepting the reality of our situation. There comes a point when instead of trying to fight death, we accept with St Francis that death is 'leading home the child of God, along the way our Lord has trod'.[195] To quote John Wyatt again:

> If our hope is in the power of medical technology to overcome every obstacle, we are doomed to ultimate disappointment. What is worse, this kind of hope may stand in the way of godly acceptance of God's will for the last phase of our life,

impeding the possibility of strengthening or 'completing' our relationships in a healthy and faithful way.[196]

Wyatt went on:

It seems sadly ironic that the effect of Christian convictions about miraculous healing can lead unintentionally to death in an intensive care unit, sedated or anaesthetized, surrounded by machinery and cared for by anonymous professionals – above all, tragically isolated from loved ones and all the possible sources of human and spiritual consolation.[197]

Dying well is inevitably a sad experience. It is sad to say goodbye to friends and loved ones. It is sad not just for the person dying, but also for friends and loved ones. I deeply regret that I did not have an opportunity to say a proper goodbye to my father, who died following a sudden massive stroke. By contrast, I have been able to tell my mother how much I love her and to thank her for being such a wonderful mother. It was tough. Tears were streaming down my face. However, as Christians we know that death does not have the last word. Death is but the gateway into the presence of God, who loves us.

Dying well involves therefore not just letting go, but also holding on to God. What is true of Christians in general needs to be true of Christian ministers too: we need to continue to exercise our faith and trust in God, holding on in faith to the faithfulness of God, who said, 'I will never leave you or forsake you' (Hebrews 13:5). The motto of Spurgeon's College, of which I was principal, comes to mind: '*teneo et teneor*' – 'I hold and I am held'.

The question arises, how can we be helped to hold on to Christ in our final hours? Some have found holding a wooden hand cross a strengthening experience, for the very emptiness of that cross speaks not just of death but also of resurrection. For others receiving Communion is an aid to faith, for as we eat bread and drink wine we look to the heavenly banquet that is to come.[198] For many hearing scripture read (such as Psalm 23; Psalm 121; John 14:1-2, 6; Revelation 21:3-4) and being prayed for can be a comforting experience. For most, however, perhaps above all what may help is the presence of a friend or loved one. To that end it has been suggested that in preparing for death we ask ourselves the question, 'Who would I like to be at my side, to embrace me as I am dying?'[199]

Although I have yet to begin the journey that leads through 'the darkest valley' (Psalm 23:4), I dare to believe that I have no reason to fear, for the Lord, the shepherd of his sheep, is with me. Yes, along with all other Christian believers, we retired ministers need to prepare for the day when all the trumpets will sound and we shall cross to the other side.[200]

A final word: making the most of your retirement

If it is my will that he remain until I come, what is that to you? Follow me!
JOHN 21:22

One of the drawbacks of this guide is that it has been very personal, for I have been using my own experience to illustrate many of the points I have been making. That has been inevitable, not least because there is so little material otherwise to draw upon. However, I am conscious that there is a danger in speaking about the way in which I am seeking to live out my call in my retirement: some could mistakenly gain the impression that I am suggesting this pattern of retirement should be the pattern for all. This, of course, is not the case. There is no one pattern. God is not in the business of cloning!

The encounter of Peter with the risen Lord is instructive. When Peter asked Jesus about what the future might hold for John, Jesus said, 'If it is my will that he remain until I come, what is that to you? Follow me' (John 21:22). Our business is to follow Jesus and not to be too concerned with anybody else. Jesus thereby implied that God has a distinctive plan for each of our lives. Diversity is a mark of God's creation; it is also a mark of his new creation. Peter died a martyr's death in Rome for his Lord in AD61; John appears to have lived to a great old age and eventually died in his sleep. Although both Peter and John followed Jesus, both ended up living very different lives. There is no one pattern for our lives. God deals with us on an individual basis and calls each of us to live out our particular calling – not least in retirement.

Hopefully the examples I have given of my retirement will cause readers to ask themselves how they in turn can apply the underlying principles to the way in which they live. Undoubtedly this will then result in many different patterns of retirement, and rightly so. My concern is that each reader will want to make the most of *their* retirement in ways which are most appropriate to their personality and gifting.

Having in my introduction quoted David Adam's inspirational poem 'The Terminus', let me end with a prayer by David Adam for all those retired people who read this book:

> *The Lord continue to extend your vision, to widen your horizons:*
> *The Lord continue to awake your senses, to deepen your*
> *   experience,*
> *that you may enter new life and go forward in joy,*
> *that you may have new ventures and continue to serve him*
> *in the power of the Almighty who makes all things new.*[201]

Notes

1 For instance, books published in the UK include Mary Hathaway, *Celebrating Retirement: A gift to mark a new beginning* (Lion, 1993); Joan Chittister, *The Gift of Years: Growing older gracefully* (DLT, 2008); David Winter, *The Highway Code for Retirement* (CWR, 2012); David Winter, *At the End of the Day: Enjoying life in the departure lounge* (BRF, 2013); Jim Packer, *Finishing Our Course with Joy: Ageing with hope* (IVP, 2014); Derek Prime, *A Good Old Age: An A to Z of loving and following the Lord Jesus in later years* (10 Publishing, 2017).

2 For instance, Paul C. Clayton, *Called for Life: Finding meaning in retirement* (Alban Institute, 2008); Gwen Wagstrom Halaas, *Clergy, Retirement, and Wholeness: Looking forward to the third age* (Alban, 2005); Daniel A. Roberts and Michael Friedman, *Clergy Retirement: Every ending a new beginning for clergy, their families and congregants* (Bayswood Publishing, 2016); also Bruce Epperly and Katherine Epperly, *Four Seasons of Ministry: Gathering a harvest of righteousness* (Alban, 2008).

3 For instance, Paul Beasley-Murray, 'Editorial: Retirement? Not yet!', *Ministry Today* 43 (Summer 2008), pp. 4–5; Jim Hamilton, 'Do ministers really retire?', *Ministry Today* 57 (Spring 2013), pp. 18–22; Paul Goodliff, 'Approaching retirement', *Ministry Today* 57 (Spring 2013), pp. 23–28; Andrew Knowles, 'Coming in to land', *Ministry Today* 59 (Autumn 2013), pp. 17–22; Paul Beasley-Murray, 'Growing old: some preliminary thoughts', *Ministry Today* 60 (Spring 2014), pp. 36–39; Keith Clements, 'Seven virtues for retired ministers', *Ministry Today* 63 (Spring 2015), pp. 40–42.

4 James Taylor, *Pastors under Pressure: Conflicts on the outside, fears within* (Day One Publications, 2nd edition 2001).

5 In the research underlying my book *Retirement Matters for Ministers: A report on a research project into how Baptist ministers experience retirement* (College of Baptist Ministers, 2018), only one-quarter of respondents said they were well prepared for retirement.

6 Os Guinness, *The Call: Finding and fulfilling the central purpose of your life* (Paternoster, 2001), pp. 243–44.

7 By contrast a 2017 Legal and General survey of 2,000 of their pensioners indicated that only 12% of their respondents mentioned 'freedom' as one of the good aspects of retirement. Other good

aspects mentioned were no time pressure (25%), hobbies (12%), grandkids/family (9%) and travelling (6%).

8 David Baker, 'Adjustments in retirement', *Baptist Ministers Journal* 293 (January 2006), p. 26, wrote: 'Emotionally I see retirement from full-time ministry like a bereavement; it is the loss of a role I have been in for a number of years. Some of the same symptoms are there: numbness, denial, anger/depression, various questionings about where we are going; then eventually comes real acceptance. I say "real" because I have had times over the past years when I thought I had accepted it but then realised I had not done so.'

9 Paul Tournier, *Learning to Grow Old* (SCM, 1960), pp. 169–70, maintained that 'acceptance of unfulfilment' is one of the great problems of the retired. He went on: 'Of God alone can the Bible say (Genesis 2:1) that on the evening of the sixth day of retirement he had completed his work.'

10 Winter, *The Highway Code for Retirement*, p. 22.

11 See Paul Beasley-Murray, *Power for God's Sake: Power and abuse in the local church* (Paternoster, 1998), pp. 47–49: on average ministers reckoned they worked 64.3 hours per week.

12 Paul Beasley-Murray, *This Is My Story: A story of life, faith, and ministry* (Wipf and Stock, 2018), p. 200.

13 The German *Ruhestand* and the French *retraite* are equally negative. However, the Spanish word for retirement, *jubilacion*, is much more positive and highlights the freedom and joy which retirement can bring.

14 Quoted by A.E. Hotchner, *Papa Hemingway: A personal memoir* (1966), part 3, ch. 12: 'The worst death for anyone is to lose the center of his being, the thing he really is. Retirement is the filthiest word in the language. Whether by choice or by fate, to retire from what you do – and makes you what you are – is to back up into the grave.'

15 See 'Ministry goes through stages' in Paul Beasley-Murray, *Living Out the Call: 1. Living to God's glory*, 2nd edition (FeedARead, 2016), pp. 89–91.

16 Epperly and Epperly, *Four Seasons of Ministry*, describe retirement as the season of winter. I think that is an unfortunate and depressing description, even though they go on to define 'winter' as 'retirement and the adventure that requires vision and letting go'. With Paul Tournier, *The Seasons of Life* (SCM, 1964). I prefer to liken retirement to the autumn of life.

17 John Keats (1795–1821), 'To Autumn': 'Season of mists and mellow fruitfulness, Close bosom-friend of the maturing sun; Conspiring with him how to load and bless, With fruit the vines that round the thatch-eves run.'
18 See Tim Stafford, *As Our Years Increase: Loving, caring, preparing – a guide* (IVP, 1989), pp. 26–28.
19 William F. May, quoted by Charles Pinches, 'The virtues of aging' in S. Hauerwas, C.B. Stoneking, Keith G. Meador and D. Cloutier (eds), *Growing Old in Christ* (Eerdmans, 2008), p. 208.
20 Nathan Davis and Beth Davis, *Finishing Well: Retirement skills for ministers*, 3rd edition (Self-published, 2008), p. 60.
21 Robert Browning, *Dramatis Personae* (1864).
22 James Woodward, *Valuing Age: Pastoral ministry with older people* (SPCK, 2008), p. 199.
23 Written by David Adam for a greeting card published by Tim Tiley, and subsequently reproduced in *Prayers As You Explore Your Vocation* (The Vocations Team of the Diocese of St Albans, 2015).
24 In his essay, 'Of Ceremonies and Respects'.
25 Chittister, *The Gift of Years*, p. 47.
26 T.S. Eliot, 'East Coker' from *Four Quartets* (Faber and Faber, 1944).
27 Richard L. Morgan, *I Never Found that Rocking Chair: God's call at retirement* (Upper Room Books, 1992), s. 74.
28 Helen Keller, *Let Us Have Faith* (Doubleday, 1940).
29 Although this line is frequently quoted on the internet, I cannot find the original source.
30 Paul Stevens, *Aging Matters: Finding your calling for the rest of your life* (Eerdmans, 2016), p. 1.
31 Camilla Cavendish, *Extra Time: Ten lessons for an ageing world* (Harper Collins, 2019), p. 33.
32 Cavendish, *Extra Time*, pp. 28–29.
33 Stafford, *As Our Years Increase*, p. 12.
34 Sharon Kaufmann, quoted by Michael Butler and Ann Orbach, *Being Your Age: Pastoral care for older people* (SPCK, 1993), p. 13.
35 Stafford, *As Our Years Increase*, pp. 26–28.
36 Eugene Bianchi, quoted by Stevens, *Aging Matters*, p. 143.
37 See Robert Collier, *The Secret of the Ages* (Martino Fine Books, 2010; reprint of 1926 original).
38 John Weaver, 'My Journey' (an unpublished paper), p. 10.
39 J. Gordon Harris, *Biblical Perspectives on Aging: God and the elderly*, 2nd edition (Hawarth/Taylor and Francis, 2008), pp. 158–59.

40 'A man is not old until regrets take the place of dreams' (John Barrymore, 1882–1942).

41 A mentor is commonly defined as a 'wise and trusted counsellor and teacher', whereas a 'soul friend' could be more of a peer.

42 See Davis and Davis, *Finishing Well*, p. 84: 'Take time to find a good mentor (or mentors) to assist you during the entering stage.'

43 Beasley-Murray, *Retirement Matters for Ministers*, p. 73.

44 John Weaver, 'A theology of retirement for ministers' (unpublished), p. 2.

45 Hamilton, 'Do ministers really retire?', p. 22.

46 See Philip Clements-Jewery, 'A retirement retreat', *Baptist Ministers' Journal* 309 (January 2011), pp. 21–22.

47 Stevens, *Aging Matters*, p. 153.

48 See Paul Beasley-Murray, *Entering New Territory: Why are retired Baptist ministers moving to Anglican churches? What are the underlying theological issues?* (College of Baptist Ministers, 2019). This report is based on a questionnaire survey of retired Baptist ministers in Anglican churches, and was sparked off by a previous survey which found that just over a quarter of retired Baptist ministers were no longer worshipping in a Baptist church: most attended Anglican churches, but some attended another free or independent church: see also Beasley-Murray, *Retirement Matters for Ministers*, p. 75.

49 Winter, *At the End of the Day*, p. 18.

50 Clements, 'Seven virtues for retired ministers', pp. 40–42.

51 Reinhold Niebuhr, *The Irony of American History* (Scribner, 1952).

52 See Paul Beasley-Murray, 'Seven virtues for retired ministers', 15 January 2015, **paulbeasleymurray.com/2015/01/15/seven-virtues-retired-ministers**.

53 Arthur A. Anderson, *Psalms*, vol. 2 (Oliphants, 1972), p. 664.

54 Artur Weiser, *The Psalms: A commentary* (SCM, 1962), p. 616.

55 Dietrich Bonhoeffer, *Life Together* (SCM, 1954), p. 53.

56 See Henri Nouwen, 'An invitation to the spiritual life', *Leadership XII* (Summer 1981), p. 57.

57 Stevens, *Aging Matters*, p. 67.

58 In my research on how Baptist ministers experience retirement, I discovered that 19% use printed Bible reading notes; 19% use online Bible reading notes; 19% read though a Bible book with a commentary; and 36% read through a Bible book without a commentary; 13% use the lectionary; and 19% reported that they

did not have a regular pattern of reading the scripture! See Beasley-Murray, *Retirement Matters for Ministers*, p. 72.

59 Cuthbert Bardsley, 'Reflections of an old man', Address to Retired Clergy Association 1985, quoted by Butler and Orbach, *Being Your Age*, p. 49.

60 H.P. Steer, *Caring for the Elderly* (SPCK, 1966), p. 32.

61 Jennifer O'Neill, '16 relationship secrets to steal from couples married for 50+ years', *Good Housekeeping*, October 2015.

62 See Beasley-Murray, *Retirement Matters for Ministers*, p. 90. Some will note that all the spouses quoted here are female. This gender imbalance reflects the fact that although the Baptist Union of Great Britain has had women ministers for over 80 years, the proportion remains relatively low. There has been an increase in recent years, but this increase has yet to reflect itself in the figures of the retired.

63 See Beasley-Murray, *Retirement Matters for Ministers*, pp. 90–91.

64 John Powell, *Why Am I Afraid To Tell You Who I Am?* (Fontana/Collins, 1975), p. 101.

65 An unpublished address given to the Baptist Union Retreat Group.

66 See Paul Beasley-Murray, 'Jesus welcomes me to come "just as I am"', 2 March 2017, **paulbeasleymurray.com/2017/03/02/jesus-welcomes-me-to-come-just-as-I-am**.

67 Beasley-Murray, *This Is My Story*, p. 201.

68 Frances van Alstyne is often known by her maiden name of Fanny Crosby.

69 Remuneration and Conditions of Service Committee of the Archbishops' Council, 'Supporting the ministry of retired clergy', first published 2007, updated 2014.

70 'Supporting the ministry of retired clergy', p. 4.

71 See Paul Goodliff, *Ministry, Sacrament and Representation: Ministry and ordination in contemporary Baptist theology, and the rise of sacramentalism* (Regent's Park College, 2010).

72 Goodliff, 'Approaching retirement', pp. 23–24.

73 Eugene Peterson, *A Long Obedience in the Same Direction: Discipleship in an instant society*, second edition (IVP, 2000).

74 Friedrich Nietzsche, *Beyond Good and Evil*, trans. Helen Zimmern (TN Foulis, 1907), s. 188.

75 I am grateful for this analogy to Canon Hugh Dibbens, who in his retirement serves as the evangelism adviser in the Barking Episcopal Area of the Diocese of Chelmsford.

76 Butler and Orbach, *Being Your Age*, p. 48.

77 Norman Jones, 'One man's retirement', *Fraternal* 190 (January 1980), p. 22, wrote of there being three types of retired ministers: 'There are those who think of their retirement as an opportunity to do more church work and get more and more absorbed in it... The second group comprises those who have retired and find liberation from everything and just enjoy retirement. The third group are of a different kind. They still love the church but see their retirement as supplying wider opportunities to join groups outside the church and to help the church see itself as others see it.'

78 Beasley-Murray, *Retirement Matters for Ministers*, p. 83.

79 Paul Beasley-Murray, 'Ministers' reading habits', *Baptist Quarterly* 49 (January 2018).

80 Beasley-Murray, *Retirement Matters for Ministers*, pp. 92–93.

81 Tournier, *Learning to Grow Old*.

82 Joseph Brodsky made this comment on the acceptance of the US poet laureateship: see *Independent on Sunday*, 19 May 1999.

83 See Rick Warren, 'To be a great leader, you absolutely must be a reader', 23 October 2014, **pastors.com/great-leader-absolutely-must-reader**.

84 C.S. Lewis, 'On the reading of old books' republished in C.S. Lewis, *Essay Collection and Other Short Pieces* (HarperCollins, 2000), p. 439. Some of these older books could well include some of the great spiritual classics of the past, such as Augustine's *Confessions*, Thomas à Kempis' *Imitation of Christ* and Julian of Norwich's *Revelations of Divine Love*.

85 Much as I love this quotation, I have recently discovered that the word 'fully' is not present in the Latin version: '*gloria enim Dei vivens homo*' (*Against Heresies* 4.20.7) – 'the glory of God is a living human being'. Irenaeus went on to say in the same sentence, '*vita autem hominis visio Dei*' ('and human life is the vision of God'). Irenaeus was not talking about making the most of what this life has to offer, but rather about the glory of encountering God.

86 Zalman Schachter-Shalomi, quoted by Rachel Kohn, 'The ageing spirit' in Elizabeth Mackinlay (ed.), *Ageing and Spirituality across Faiths and Cultures* (Jessica Kingsley, 2010), p. 64. See also Woodward, *Valuing Age*, p. 192: 'Wisdom is not what you know about; it is what you know, deep inside you, the essence of your inner life. Wisdom is the art of holding together the old and the new, of balancing the known with the unknown, the pain and the joy; it is a way of linking the whole of your life together in a needful integrity.'

87 Richard Rohr, *Falling Upward: A spirituality for the two halves of life* (SPCK, 2011), p. xxv.

88 Rohr, *Falling Upward*, pp. 138, 160.

89 Daniel Estes, *Hear, My Son: Teaching and learning in Proverbs 1–9* (Apollos, 1997), p. 134. See also Nan Thomas and Thomas Trevethan, 'A Christian theology of mentoring', InterVarsity Christian Fellowship, 2018, **gfm.intervarsity.org/resources/christian-theology-mentoring**.

90 Tournier, *Learning to Grow Old*, p. 198.

91 See W. Charles Johnson, 'What can a retired minister contribute to the church?', *Fraternal* 167 (May 1973), p. 31: 'A retired minister's ministry should be essentially a ministry of encouragement and in particular of younger men.' See also Paul Beasley-Murray, 'Encourage your minister', *Ministry Today* 55 (Summer 1992).

92 William James, 'Letter to his class of Radcliffe College, 6 April 1896' in *Letters, Vol. 2* (Longmans, Green and Co, 1920), p. 23.

93 Beasley-Murray, *Retirement Matters for Ministers*, p. 76.

94 This comment by Larry Moyer, in *A Mentor's Wisdom: Lessons I learned from Haddon Robinson* (Hendrickson, Peabody, 2018), p. 16, has been taken out of context. The author's concern was 'to make it a point to speak a word of praise to someone each day'.

95 Although John Piper does not use this language, this is essentially the thrust of his booklet *Rethinking Retirement: Finishing life for the glory of Christ* (Crossway, 2009).

96 Fred Craddock, *Philippians* (John Knox, 1985), p. 62.

97 Ben Witherington III, *Letters and Homilies for Jewish Christians: A socio-rhetorical commentary on Hebrews, James and Jude* (Apollos, 2007), p. 327: 'When combined with *eis*, the verb *aphorountes* in Hebrews 12:2 means a definite looking away from other things and a fixing of one's eyes on only the goal.'

98 Peter T. O'Brien, *The Letter to the Hebrews* (Eerdmans, 2010), p. 453.

99 O'Brien, *The Letter to the Hebrews*, p. 453 n. 33.

100 William L. Lane, *Hebrews 9—13* (Word, 1991), p. 410.

101 Lane, *Hebrews 9—13*, p. 410.

102 An extract from her BBC Radio 4 sermon given on 3 March 2010, and quoted in John Weaver, 'Hopeful disciples in a time of climate change' in Stephen Finamore and John Weaver (eds), *Wisdom, Science, and the Scriptures: Essays in honour of Ernest Lucas* (Wipf and Stock, 2014), pp. 134–55.

103 Winter, *The Highway Code for Retirement*, p. 22.

104   Winter, *The Highway Code for Retirement*, p. 100.

105   Woodward, *Valuing Age*, p. 199.

106   Jaco Hamman, 'Playing' in Bonnie J. Miller-McLemore (ed), *The Wiley-Blackwell Companion to Practical Theology* (Blackwell, 2012), p. 42.

107   Hamman, 'Playing', p. 49.

108   Rodney Macready, *Retiring Retirement* (Hendrickson, 2016). See also Paul Stevens, who began his book *Aging Matters* with the provocative statement, 'We should work until we die' (p. 11): 'Scripture from Genesis to Revelation affirms that work is a critical part of what it means to be a human being in the image of God… Work is energy expended *purposively*' (p. 18, italics in original).

109   Macready, *Retiring Retirement*, p. 3.

110   Macready, *Retiring Retirement*, p. 220.

111   Morgan, *I Never Found That Rocking Chair*, s. 74.

112   Cavendish, *Extra Time*, p. 48.

113   **thegospelcoalition.org/blogs/erik-raymond/so-why-are-pastors-fat**

114   See Paul Beasley-Murray, 'Why are so many ministers fat?', 31 March 2014, **paulbeasleymurray.com/2014/04/10/why-are-so-many-ministers-fat**.

115   **ageuk.org.uk/information-advice/health-wellbeing/exercise/walking-tips-advice**

116   Beasley-Murray, *Retirement Matters for Ministers*, p. 70.

117   Lord Stanley, later 15th Earl of Derby, was secretary of state for foreign affairs 1866–68 and 1874–78.

118   See Paul Beasley-Murray, 'Levels of friendship', 21 June 2018, **paulbeasleymurray.com/2018/06/21/levels-of-friendship**. See also Kaya Burgess, 'A stranger can become your friend in 90 hours', *The Times*, 14 April 2018.

119   See, for instance, *Age UK Loneliness Review* (revised July 2015), which cites S. Pettigrew, R. Donovan, D. Boldy, and R. Newton, 'Older people's perceived causes of and strategies for dealing with social isolation', *Aging and Mental Health* 18 (2014), pp. 914–20.

120   Chittister, *The Gift of Years*, p. 79.

121   Quoted in *The Times*, 14 April 2018.

122   Winter, *The Highway Code for Retirement*, p. 44.

123   Horace Walpole, Letter CCLII (252) in *The Letters of Horace Walpole, Early of Oxford, to Sir Horace Mann*, Volume 1 (Lea and Blanchard, 1844), p. 406.

124 A.W. Plumstead and Harrison Hayford (eds), *The Journals and Miscellaneous Notebooks of Ralph Waldo Emerson, Vol. 7 (1838–1842)* (Harvard University Press, 1969), p. 61.

125 A phrase found in his 1980 musical *Merrily We Roll Along*.

126 Art Linklater, quoted by Gene Perret, *Grandchildren Are So Much Fun, We Should Have Them First* (Arizona Highways, 2001).

127 Jay Kessler, *Grandparenting: The agony and the ecstasy* (Hodder and Stoughton, 1994).

128 Kessler, *Grandparenting*, p. 29.

129 Kessler, *Grandparenting*, p. 31.

130 Kessler, *Grandparenting*, p. 116.

131 Kessler, *Grandparenting*, p. 72.

132 Kessler, *Grandparenting*, p. 81.

133 Paul Beasley-Murray, 'Editorial: The challenge of Christian grandparenting', *Ministry Today* 69 (Spring 2017), pp. 3–7.

134 The verses were John 3:16; Psalm 23:1; Psalm 121:2; Matthew 7:12; Matthew 28:20; Mark 10:43; John 8:12; John 13:34; 1 Corinthians 13:4; Galatians 2:20; Philippians 4:6; and Hebrews 13:8.

135 See Beasley-Murray, *Retirement Matters for Ministers*, pp. 91–92.

136 Beasley-Murray, *This is My Story*, p. xv.

137 Epperly and Epperly, *Four Seasons of Ministry*, pp. 174–75.

138 Two such journals are *Dear Grandad, from Me to You: Memory journal capturing your own grandfather's amazing stories* and *Dear Grandma, from Me to You: Memory journal capturing your own grandmother's amazing stories* (Journals of a Lifetime, 2017). Each journal contains over 60 questions and prompts to help grandparents write about their childhood.

139 See Win and Charles Arn, 'Catching the age wave', *Faith and Renewal* (September–October 1993), pp. 23–28. Also 'The age wave is here', *Church Growth Digest* 12 (Spring 1991), pp. 3–5.

140 Vernon Grounds, 'A personal perspective', in C. Ben Mitchell, Robert D. Orr and Susan A. Salladay (eds), *Aging, Death and the Quest for Immortality* (Eerdmans, 2004), pp. 3–13.

141 Daniel Taylor, *Tell Me a Story: The life-shaping power of our stories* (Bog Walk, 2001; previously published as *The Healing Power of Stories*, Doubleday, 1996), p. 1.

142 Leslie Farber, *The Ways of the Will: Selected essays* (Basic Books, 2000), pp. 9–10.

143 See Nathan Kirkpatrick, who draws on Henning Mankell and John Niles, **faithandleadership.com/nathan-kirkpatrick-tell-it-again**.

144 Richard Kearney, *On Stories* (Routledge, 2002), p. 156.

145 Quoted by James Roose-Evans, *Passages of the Soul: Rituals today* (Element, 1994), pp. xiii–xiv.

146 Woodward, *Valuing Age*, p. 204.

147 Woodward, *Valuing Age*, p. 205.

148 Thomas Merton, *No Man Is an Island* (Shambhala Publications, 2005), p. 73.

149 Tournier, *The Seasons of Life*, p. 54.

150 Tournier, *Learning to Grow Old*, pp. 204–5.

151 Clayton, *Called for Life*, p. 88.

152 Clayton, *Called for Life*, p. 97.

153 The image here is the exact reverse of the plot in Oscar Wilde's novel *The Picture of Dorian Gray*, in which the vain Dorian Gray has his portrait painted, and when it is finished he laments: 'How sad! I shall grow old and horrible, but this picture never will be older. If it were I was to be always young, and the picture that was to grow old, I would give my soul for that!' But as Dorian Gray discovered, there is more to life than looks. Just as vintage wine has much to be desired, so too has an older person who has grown in grace. In words attributed to Michelangelo: 'The more the marble wastes, the more the statue grows.'

154 Winter, *At the End of the Day*, p. 47. See also Pope John XXIII, *Journal of a Soul*: 'Above all I must endeavour to keep myself in serene and loving converse with him.'

155 Gordon Rupp, 'Growing younger', *The Sixty Plus and Other Sermons* (Fount/Collins, 1978), pp. 12–13.

156 This prayer, often said to be from the 17th century, is more likely to be a 20th-century creation.

157 Quoted by William Barclay, *The Letters to the Philippians, Colossians and Thessalonians – The New Daily Study Bible* (Saint Andrew Press, 1975).

158 G. Walter Hansen, *The Letter to the Philippians* (Apollos, 2009), p. 310.

159 Winter, *At the End of the Day*, pp. 128–29, quoting Richard Ingrams, *Muggeridge: The biography* (Harper Collins, 1995).

160 This prayer was adopted by Alcoholics Anonymous. It is not widely known that at the same time Niebuhr wrote a second prayer to accompany his original prayer, setting the serenity prayer within a specifically Christian context, which some might well find more helpful:

Living one day at a time,
Enjoying one moment at a time,
Accepting hardship as a pathway to peace,
Taking, as Jesus did,
This sinful world as it is,
Not as I would have it,
Trusting that You will make all things right,
If I surrender to Your will,
So that I may be reasonably happy in this life,
And supremely happy with You forever in the next.

161 I have lost the source of this quotation.
162 See Cicely Saunders, 'Care of the dying – 1. The problem of euthanasia', *Nursing Times* (1976), pp. 1003–5.
163 Carl Jung, *Memories, Dreams, Reflections*, edited by Aniela Jaffe (Fontana, 1995).
164 Francis Bridger, *23 Days: A story of love, death and God* (DLT, 2004), p. 32.
165 Bridger, *23 Days*, p. 119.
166 Beasley-Murray, *Retirement Matters for Ministers*, p. 70.
167 Beasley-Murray, *Retirement Matters for Ministers*, p. 71.
168 Beasley-Murray, *Retirement Matters for Ministers*, p. 71.
169 Bill Kirkpatrick, *Going Forth: A practical and spiritual approach to dying and death* (DLT, 1997), p. 85.
170 Written by L.J. Egerton Smith, it was a hymn Caroline and I chose for our wedding.
171 John Bunyan's pilgrim's hymn.
172 Written by Christopher Idle, it is a modern paraphrase of Psalm 18.
173 Kirkpatrick, *Going Forth*, pp. 82–83.
174 James F. White, *Introduction to Christian Worship* (Abingdon, 1980), p. 270. He added: 'Members of one retirement home weave their own funeral palls, a magnificent final affirmation.'
175 Clayton, *Called for Life*, p. 97.
176 Pope John XXIII said these words to his physician just before he died on 3 June 1963.
177 John Baillie, *The Sense of the Presence of God: 1961 Gifford Lectures* (Oxford University Press, 1962). See Colossians 3:15–16.
178 Epperly and Epperly, *Four Seasons of Ministry*, p. 176.
179 Epperly and Epperly, *Four Seasons of Ministry*, p. 176.
180 John Stott, *The Message of the Sermon on the Mount* (IVP, 1978), pp. 149–50.

181 C.S. Lewis, *Fern-Seed and Elephants* (Fount, 1998), pp. 42–43.
Desmond Tutu, in his role as head of the South African Truth
and Reconciliation Commission (which was set up to encourage
reconciliation between former victims and their oppressors), said,
'It is not enough to let bygones be bygones. Indeed just saying
that ensures it will not be so. Reconciliation does not come easy.
Believing it does not ensure that it will ever be. We have to work
and look the beast firmly in the eyes. Ultimately you discover
that without forgiveness there is no future' – cited by Terri Spy,
'Christianity, therapy and forgiveness', in Cynthia Ransley and Terri
Spy (eds), *Forgiveness and the Healing Process: A central therapeutic
concern* (Brunner-Routledge, 2004), p. 39.

182 Helmut Thielicke, *Our Heavenly Father: Sermons on the Lord's Prayer*
(Harper, 1960), p. 110.

183 Scholars debate whether these words belonged to the original
text of Luke, for these words are absent from some manuscripts.
Most commentators, however, believe that Luke did indeed pen
these words of Jesus, but that a later copyist omitted them on the
grounds that he felt that God could never have forgiven the Jews for
crucifying the Saviour – for him as for many other early Christians
the fall and destruction of Jerusalem in AD70 was a clear sign that
God did not forgive the Jews.

184 William H. Willimon, *Thank God It's Friday: Encountering the seven
last words from the cross* (Abingdon, 2006), pp. 5–6.

185 The story is told by Spy, 'Christianity, therapy and forgiveness', p. 38.

186 See Dewey Bertolini, *Secret Wounds and Silent Cries* (Victor/Scripture
Press, 1993), p. 42.

187 Margaret Magdalen, *Jesus – Man of Prayer* (Hodder and Stoughton,
1987), p. 136.

188 See also Desmond Tutu in his foreword to Marina Cantacuzino, *The
Forgiveness Project: Stories for a vengeful age* (Jessica Kingsley,
2015): 'To forgive is not just to be altruistic; in my view it is a form of
self-interest. The process of forgiving does not exclude hatred and
anger. These emotions are all part of being human. When I talk of
forgiveness, I mean the ability to let go of the right to revenge and to
slip the chains of rage that bind you to the person who harmed you.
When you forgive, you are free of the hatred and anger that locks
you in a state of victimhood. If you can find it in yourself to forgive,
you can move on, and may even help the perpetrator to become a
better person.'

189 See Paul Beasley-Murray, 'A sermon idea for the funeral of a person suffering from dementia', *Ministry Today* 71 (Autumn 2017), pp. 42–43.

190 Quoted by Mark Oakley, *Readings for Funerals* (SPCK, 2015), p. 66.

191 'Death has a sharper sting for the faithful', *The Times*, 31 October 2018, p. 13.

192 See Kathryn Mannix, *With the End in Mind: Dying, death, and wisdom in an age of denial* (William Collins, 2017), p. 5: 'By encountering death many thousands of times, I have come to a view there is usually little to fear and much to prepare for.' This does not, however, rule out the need for courage: 'Rather than performing brave deeds, courage may involve living bravely, as life ebbs. Or it may involve embarking on a conversation that feels very uncomfortable, and yet enables someone to feel accompanied in their darkness' (p. 15).

193 David Frampton, 'Caring for those struggling with terminal illness', *Ministry Today* 68 (Summer 2006), pp. 16–18.

194 John Wyatt, *Dying Well* (IVP, 2018), p. 15.

195 From the hymn 'All creatures of our God and king' by W.H. Draper (1855–1933) based on 'The Canticle of the Sun' by Francis of Assisi (1182–1226). Literally Francis wrote: 'Praised be You, my Lord, through our Sister Bodily Death, from whom no living man can escape' (Laudato si mi Signore, per sora nostra Morte corporale, da la quale nullu homo uiuente pò skappare).

196 Wyatt, *Dying Well*, p. 64.

197 Wyatt, *Dying Well*, p. 66.

198 See Paul Beasley-Murray, 'Ritual with the dying', *Living Out the Call: 4. Serving God's people*, revised edition (FeedARead, 2016), pp. 44–45.

199 Kirkpatrick, *Going Forth*, p. 10.

200 See John Bunyan, *The Pilgrim's Progress* (Collins, 1953), p. 317: 'After this it was noised abroad, that Mister Valiant-for-Truth was taken with a summons and had this for a token that the summons was true, "That his pitcher was broken at the fountain." When he understood it, he called for his friends, and told them of it. Then said he, "I am going to my Father's, and though with great difficulty I am got hither, yet now I do not repent me of all the trouble I have been at to arrive where I am. My sword, I give to him that shall succeed me in my pilgrimage, and my courage and skill, to him that can get it. My marks and scars I carry with me, a witness for me, that

I have fought, who now will be my rewarded." When the day that he must go hence was come, many accompanied him to the riverside, into which, as he went, he said, "Death, where is thy sting?" And as he went down deeper, he said, "Grave where is thy victory?" So he passed over, and all the trumpets sounded for him on the other side.'

201   'Retirement: a new beginning', written by David Adam for a greeting card published by Tim Tiley.